The
WOMEN
of
Microsoft

The
WOMEN
of
Microsoft

The
WOMEN
of
Microsoft

{ Empowering Stories from the Minds that **Coded the World** }

MIRI RODRIGUEZ & IZABELA DUIWE

WILEY

Copyright © 2025 by John Wiley & Sons, Inc. All rights reserved, including rights for text and data mining and training of artificial technologies or similar technologies.

Published by John Wiley & Sons, Inc., Hoboken, New Jersey.
Published simultaneously in Canada.

No part of this publication may be reproduced, stored in a retrieval system, or transmitted in any form or by any means, electronic, mechanical, photocopying, recording, scanning, or otherwise, except as permitted under Section 107 or 108 of the 1976 United States Copyright Act, without either the prior written permission of the Publisher, or authorization through payment of the appropriate per-copy fee to the Copyright Clearance Center, Inc., 222 Rosewood Drive, Danvers, MA 01923, (978) 750-8400, fax (978) 750-4470, or on the web at www.copyright.com. Requests to the Publisher for permission should be addressed to the Permissions Department, John Wiley & Sons, Inc., 111 River Street, Hoboken, NJ 07030, (201) 748-6011, fax (201) 748-6008, or online at http://www.wiley.com/go/permission.

Trademarks: Wiley and the Wiley logo are trademarks or registered trademarks of John Wiley & Sons, Inc. and/or its affiliates in the United States and other countries and may not be used without written permission. All other trademarks are the property of their respective owners. John Wiley & Sons, Inc. is not associated with any product or vendor mentioned in this book.

Limit of Liability/Disclaimer of Warranty: While the publisher and author have used their best efforts in preparing this book, they make no representations or warranties with respect to the accuracy or completeness of the contents of this book and specifically disclaim any implied warranties of merchantability or fitness for a particular purpose. No warranty may be created or extended by sales representatives or written sales materials. The advice and strategies contained herein may not be suitable for your situation. You should consult with a professional where appropriate. Further, readers should be aware that websites listed in this work may have changed or disappeared between when this work was written and when it is read. Neither the publisher nor authors shall be liable for any loss of profit or any other commercial damages, including but not limited to special, incidental, consequential, or other damages.

For general information on our other products and services or for technical support, please contact our Customer Care Department within the United States at (800) 762-2974, outside the United States at (317) 572-3993 or fax (317) 572-4002.

Wiley also publishes its books in a variety of electronic formats. Some content that appears in print may not be available in electronic formats. For more information about Wiley products, visit our website at www.wiley.com.

Library of Congress Cataloging-in-Publication Data is Available:

ISBN 9781394342808 (Cloth)
ISBN 9781394342815 (ePub)
ISBN 9781394342822 (ePDF)

Cover Design: Wiley
Cover Image: © Annaspoka/Getty Images

SKY10119828_062825

To the Shemothers who led with courage and the future Shes who will rise—may we continue to empower one another, and the world, with code and confidence.

Contents

Foreword ix
Introduction xiii

1 She, the People 1
2 All Roads Lead to Microsoft 23
3 Dream House 41
4 Diversity: Damned If You Do, Damned If You Don't 61
5 Resilience and the Bias Monster 77
6 Tell Your Story, or Someone Else Will 95
7 Let's Laugh at Perfectionism 113
8 Stay On Fire but Don't Burn Out 129
9 Learn-HER-Alls 145
10 Fitting Room—Leadership Comes in All Shapes and Sizes 165
11 Get That Promotion 187
12 To Microsoft and Beyond 205
13 Portrait Gallery 227

Notes 237
Acknowledgements 245
About the Authors 247
Index 249

Foreword

Making four grown men cry at 10 am on a Tuesday morning was not on my bingo card, but there you go.

My fellow engineering manager colleagues and I were at the Mexico City Microsoft office, doing our annual hiring trip where we attempted to find the best engineers from the top universities in Mexico. We wanted to hire them to work on the Windows and Office teams at Microsoft.

We'd been on these recruiting trips for eight years in a row at this point. Very few things surprised us. We had hired some incredible talent who always brought top-notch code skills but ALSO very unique points-of-view on how to make our products better for everyone in the world. Our hiring rates were around 80%—very high for the tech industry—because of how talented and technical the engineering students were.

This Tuesday though . . . things went in a VERY different direction.

I was the first interviewer for a young woman. Let's call her Yulia. She walked into the room, looking quite scared and like she really wished she could be anywhere else.

My Spanish is fairly god-awful but I attempted a round of "Holas" and "Como estas" and such.

I asked her about her background, then tossed her my starter coding question (the one that most students can do—so it helps put them at ease). In that moment she blossomed. She grabbed the marker and slammed code on the board so fast, I was taken aback at the transformation.

Happy at how she had visibly relaxed, I gave her my medium question. She finished that PLUS test cases in three minutes.

Wow. I then gave her my hardest question, the one most college students don't get without hints.

She wrote the algorithm, wrote the code, wrote the test cases like it was the easiest thing she'd done that day.

Impressed, I asked her to sit down and tell me her story.

Turned out that she lived in a remote village outside Mexico City. To learn coding during high school, she used to walk to the nearest town, about five miles away. There she would use old Java books people had thrown into the recycle bins and the library computers to teach herself to code. For a long time, she only coded on paper at home to work out problems in real time.

When she saw Microsoft was recruiting at her university, she applied for a job. Many students around her said, "You'll never get that job. You don't even speak English."

So she started practicing English by watching YouTube videos every night.

I was fairly shocked when I stumbled back into the deliberation room to tell my four colleagues this story.

Reader: my colleagues and I hired her. She was our top candidate that year.

When she got the offer we cried as much as she did.

And yes, she's crushing it to this day.

Yulia is such an example of having unwavering belief in the ability to figure things out. So many women in Microsoft have this belief. These women have raised me during my entire 20-year career at Microsoft. Without women like Yulia to lift me up on both the good days and bad days, I would be nowhere.

I am so grateful to Miri Rodriguez and Izabela Duiwe for collecting stories from so many of us to share with you all. It's these origin stories that make up the fabric of what it's like to work at Microsoft and what has made the company so special and so impactful.

Happy 50th birthday, Microsoft.

Let's keep doing the thing and changing lives all over the world.

—Dona Sarkar,
Chief Troublemaker, Microsoft AI,
Copilot and Agents

Introduction

It all started with a ping.

One random spring day, Izzy reached out to me over Teams—just another message in the endless scroll of notifications. She wanted some advice about an idea she had for a book. So, I did what I always do when a fellow woman at Microsoft reaches out: I jumped on a call. We talked about her vision, her hopes, and her "why." But what I didn't expect—what completely knocked me sideways—was that by the end of that call, she'd ask me to co-author it with her.

Now, I know that might sound pretty ordinary—two colleagues connecting over a project. But here's the thing: if we pause for just a moment, if we lean in and really unpack what happened, we start to see the magic. This is the story of the *She*.

Picture it: Izzy in Poland, me miles away from sunny Miami, two women who had never met in person. And yet, because we're women at Microsoft, because this company fosters connection and creates spaces for us to find one another, and because the technology Microsoft creates bridges distances and time zones like never before, we were able to meet—and from that simple conversation, a friendship was born. And so was this book.

That moment—that small, ordinary moment—is the heartbeat of this book. It's about women with big dreams, working in a male-dominated industry, daring to do something they've never done before. It's about trusting that quiet voice inside that says, "This is bigger than you. This isn't just about *you*. This is about legacy." It's about the courage to show up, even when the outcome is uncertain, because you know the impact could ripple across generations.

This book is a love letter to the women of Microsoft, of the tech industry and beyond—to their journeys, their triumphs, their heartbreaks, and their resilience. It's a testament to the fact that we're not alone in our quest for more: more purpose, more connection, more belonging. Through these stories, we hope you find not just inspiration, but practical wisdom for navigating your own path. And maybe, just maybe, you'll see yourself reflected in these pages.

Here's what's waiting for you:

Chapter 1: She, the People

> Step back into the early days of personal computing and meet the women who helped shape Microsoft's products, culture, and influence. As you turn each page, you'll discover the unsung pioneers whose fingerprints are all over the technology you use every day—and perhaps even see how their stories mirror your own.

Chapter 2: All Roads Lead to Microsoft

> You'll journey through the winding, unexpected paths that brought diverse women—technical and non-technical—to Microsoft. Their stories of setbacks, pivots, and triumphs will remind you that success isn't a straight line, and your unique path is part of what makes you extraordinary.

Chapter 3: Dream House

> Imagine Microsoft as a house. In this chapter, you'll explore how women have claimed every room, transforming spaces into places of belonging and creativity. You'll see how you, too, can make your mark in every corner of your life and work.

Chapter 4: Diversity: Damned If You Do, Damned If You Don't

This chapter invites you into a raw, unfiltered conversation about diversity, equity, and inclusion. Beyond the buzzwords, you'll explore what it really means to live these values in a corporate world—and how your voice can contribute to meaningful change.

Chapter 5: Resilience and the Bias Monster

Here, you'll meet courageous women who stood their ground against prejudice. As you read their stories, you'll find inspiration to turn your own challenges into stepping-stones and face your own Bias Monsters with resilience and grace.

Chapter 6: Tell Your Story, or Someone Else Will

This chapter is a heartfelt invitation to own your story—the messy, beautiful, imperfect chapters—and find joy in the narrative you're crafting. Because if you don't tell your story, someone else will. And no one can tell it like you.

Chapter 7: Let's Laugh at Perfectionism

Get ready to laugh—and maybe shed a tear—as you read the stories from women who broke free from the suffocating grip of perfectionism. You'll discover that there's freedom in the mess, and that embracing imperfection can be your greatest superpower.

Chapter 8: Stay On Fire but Don't Burn Out

Join honest conversations about pursuing your passions without sacrificing your well-being. You'll learn how to fuel your fire without burning out—because burnout isn't a badge of honor, and your well-being matters.

Chapter 9: Learn-HER-Alls

> Dive into the journey of becoming a lifelong learner and see how Microsoft's culture of growth—nurtured under Satya Nadella's leadership—has empowered women to thrive personally and professionally. You'll find practical tools to embrace change and growth in your own life.

Chapter 10: Fitting Room—Leadership Comes in All Shapes and Sizes

> Step into the fitting room of leadership and explore lessons from women who have redefined what it means to lead. You'll see how embracing authenticity over outdated molds can help you develop your own unique leadership style.

Chapter 11: Get That Promotion

> Be inspired by the bold, risky steps women took to climb the corporate ladder. Their stories of triumph and hard-earned wisdom will give you the courage to take your own leaps and navigate the costs and benefits along the way.

Chapter 12: To Microsoft and Beyond

> Meet the trailblazers who are shaping the next 50 years of technology—from AI and Quantum to Mesh and Cloud. Their stories will ignite your imagination about the future and show you how to be a part of it.

Chapter 13: Portrait Gallery

> In our final section, we celebrate the 50 extraordinary women at Microsoft who contributed to this book, as the company marks its 50th anniversary.
>
> We hope you enjoy reading these stories as much as we have enjoyed writing them!

Chapter 1

She, the People

A woman with a voice is by definition a strong woman . . .
—Melinda Gates

In the dynamic world of technology, two skills stand out as essential for women to master: code and confidence. One is a mix of languages, each with its own syntax and beauty, waiting for eager *left-brainiacs* to unravel their mysteries. The other, well, this one feels more like an ancient, cryptic script—full of wisdom, yet challenging for any mind to decipher and even more so to embody.

Throughout my career in tech, I've seen many women navigate code with grace and skill, mastering its complexities. Yet, the journey to true confidence feels less traveled, its path not as clear. Coding offers a more visible trail; its concepts are more concrete. For those of us not immersed in algorithms or debugging, the basics of coding seem surprisingly approachable. The steps are straightforward, inviting you to choose your preferred language and begin your coding adventure.

1. **Prepare Your Environment:** Cultivate a space where your digital creations will take root.
2. **Write Your First Lines:** Let your thoughts flow into the structure of code.

3. **Compile with Precision:** Sharpen your creation, transforming it into a form the machine understands.

4. **Run and Observe:** Bring your code to life and marvel at its first breath.

5. **Understand and Grow:** Absorb the essence of each command, each misstep, and each triumph.

And with the dawn of AI, this journey has become even more accessible. Engage with an AI in your natural tongue, and voilà—a *Hello World!* greets you, as if by magic. The bridge between human intention and digital expression has never been shorter. Yet, when it comes to confidence, the path leads us into a less-traveled alley. Unlike the varied programming languages, confidence is a singular, nuanced dialect that every woman I've met—myself included—strives to speak fluently. It's a language whispered through generations, delicately woven into the fabric of life's success, but it carries no clear method for mastery. We approach it with caution, unsure of whom to ask for guidance or where to even start.

Over the past decade, I've mentored a multitude of women, many of whom share a common inquiry: "How can I cultivate confidence?" Occasionally, the question is more personal: "How did you gain your confidence?" The initial time I encountered this question, it caught me off guard—I hadn't perceived myself as someone who exuded confidence. This prompted a moment—ok, many moments—of introspection and with a hint of amusement, I began to delve into the depths of my own path to becoming fluent in the language of self-assurance and to think deeply about those pivotal moments that rendered me bilingual.

In my reflections, I often consider the deliberate steps our ancient foremothers might have taken to emerge as paragons of courage and determination. On their ascent to leadership, I'd like to think that they cultivated their *ladyboss* catwalk with the same deliberate care as a developer crafts their first lines of code, to extract the profound language of badassery accessible and resonant for all of us who sought to follow in their footsteps.

Indulge me for a minute. Let's journey to 1975 New Mexico, where the air hums with The Captain and Tennille's "Love Will Keep Us Together," and cinema halls echo with the suspense of *Jaws*. Amidst the poignant return of Vietnam troops and a cultural scene in flux, Andrea Lewis finds herself in deep conversation with her mother, in frank discussions with peers, and sharing heartfelt thoughts with trusted confidants as she contemplates joining an embryonic tech startup as a technical writer. While it may be a flight of fancy, there's a universal nod to the audacity of a woman joining a fledging software company as Employee Number 5 during a time when women's presence in tech was scarce. Andrea Lewis's seemingly inconspicuous decision was, in reality, a giant step for womankind. Whether Lewis or any other trailblazing woman at Microsoft cultivated their confidence prior to stepping into the tech arena, or if it was the very act of stepping in that necessitated the cultivation of such confidence, remains a question. Nevertheless, as she navigated and decoded the complexities of a male-dominated field, she didn't just write code; she rewrote history. Or as some like to better call it: HERstory.

Indeed, it's all about the She.

She is the less than 1% of women who graduated from engineering in the 1970s. She is the mere 8% of STEM women workers who faced a stark wage gap, earning only 59 cents to every dollar earned by their male counterparts. She is every woman at Microsoft, from Employee 5 to Employee Number 221,000—and all those in between—who has boldly donned her "big girl boots" to navigate the challenging terrain of injustice, prejudice, discrimination, and the persistent frustration of inequality. She has not only walked this path but has blazed a trail for other women to follow. She continues to take significant strides, forging a future where the next generation can walk with less resistance and more recognition. Her journey is one of relentless determination, of code and confidence.

For the last 50 years, the She of Microsoft has been the architect of change, her every decision contributing to the trillion-dollar, most valuable and innovative company in the world we know today. She has been in code rooms, and board rooms. She has cried in bathrooms and laughed in chat rooms. She has broken designer heels on the headquarters' concrete floors and broken through glass ceilings with the design of new technologies that revolutionized the way we live and work. She has been the silent force behind major launches and the loud cheer in company celebrations. From the early days of punch cards to the era of cloud computing, she has been there, coding not just software, but a future of inclusivity and innovation.

She has mentored interns and managed teams, juggled deadlines with daycare drop-offs, and faced biases during menopause. She has been the first to arrive and the last to leave. Her fingerprints are on patents, her ideas in products, her vision in the company's road map. She is the unsung hero and the celebrated leader, the quiet contributor and the vocal advocate. Indeed, her very presence is a declaration of confidence. Each day she arrives, she silently decodes the age-old scripts of self-assurance, teaching us through her perseverance what it means to be a woman of confidence.

She is every woman at Microsoft—past, present, and future—who has dared to dream, to challenge, to create, and to lead. Her story is Microsoft's story, but is also every woman's story: a narrative of perseverance, empowerment, and groundbreaking achievements that continue to inspire and shape the world.

It's our profound privilege to bring these scripts to light, to allow the language of confidence to be spoken openly and joyfully, echoing as a celebration of every woman's journey.

We move beyond conjecture about the beginnings of her bold choices; we dissect the nuances of her decisions, gleaning wisdom from each deliberate move. This insight does more than just inform—it inspires. It equips us to be the foremothers who light the way for the She who will follow, ensuring that the path of confidence is well trodden and inviting for the generations to come.

Let's begin.

From the beginning, Microsoft's journey has been one of remarkable skill and unshaken confidence. Along the way, its milestones, challenges, and triumphs have echoed the life experiences of countless women—including those at Microsoft—some of whom I've had the privilege of mentoring in building their personal brands, and some of whom we are honoring within the pages of this book.

When women look back on their paths to achievement, confidence often shines as a key ingredient. But looming in the background is a relentless foe—Imposter Syndrome—eroding self-belief and thwarting chances. Not to be confused with the Bias Monster, which we will talk about in Chapter 5, this persistent enemy is widely acknowledged as a significant barrier to career progression for women in the workplace.[1] And if you're like me, no matter how much you try to silence it, it never seems to vanish completely.

I sometimes wonder if Bill Gates or Paul Allen ever struggled with Imposter Syndrome. I'm willing to bet they did. It's a universal experience. They surely faced failure. When asked about having the confidence to succeed, Gates once advised: "It's fine to celebrate success, but it is more important to heed the lessons of failure."[2] Ok, Bill. Tell us more! What can we learn about failure from a company that transformed itself from a humble garage startup into a trillion-dollar powerhouse, earning the title of Most Valuable Company in the World—twice?

Webster's Dictionary defines confidence as an awareness of one's abilities or reliance on circumstances. ChatGPT describes it as a belief in one's capabilities, worth, or judgment, while Copilot sees it as a multifaceted trait. Despite their nuances, these definitions agree on one thing: confidence springs from two sources—internal and external.

> **Internal or Self-Belief:** This involves a profound sense of your abilities and intrinsic worth, propelling you to tackle challenges and pursue your goals with unwavering determination.
>
> **External or Circumstantial Assurance:** Confidence is also shaped by external factors such as supportive environments, past successes, and positive feedback from others, all of which reinforce your internal self-belief.

Let's chat about Microsoft's journey—a tale of boldness, innovation, and sheer determination, even in the face of setbacks. There's certainly much to learn from this tech giant's five decades of visionary leaders, adaptability under competitive pressure, and fearless exploration of new frontiers, as well as how the She of each decade empowered herself to become a trailblazer and giant in her own right.

Microsoft was born in 1975 when Bill Gates and Paul Allen, two young visionaries who believed in the transformative power of software, dared to imagine a world shaped by their vision, planting the seeds for a future full of innovation. Belief is such a powerful word, and dare I say, the key ingredient to confidence. It means trusting in the potential of your ideas, the value of your contributions, and having unseen faith in your capacity to achieve and overcome obstacles. Easier said than done, I know. Studies indicate that women, even high-achievers, often have less confidence than men in certain subjects, such as math, and are more likely to downplay their own abilities.[3]

I'm not exactly sure when it happened, but there was a pivotal moment in my life when I transitioned from an *"I-can-be-and-do-anything-I-want"* girl to an *"I-don't-even-know-who-I-am"* woman. And that was the fateful day I first met Imposter Syndrome. I began questioning my abilities, my style, even my smile. Did I smile too much? Or not enough? I wore heels to boost my confidence, only to receive critical stares for my choice of wardrobe. Ugh. How I hated those days—and the length of time it took me to learn to ignore Imposter Syndrome once and for all.

Research suggests that both biological and environmental factors influence confidence levels in girls. If we were to explore just one factor, such as social media, we could fill this entire book—and more—to gain a deep understanding on the profound impact this technology has had on girls' and women's confidence levels. As a member of Generation X, I'm secretly grateful that social media emerged when I was well into my 20s. I can't imagine what Millennials and Generation Z have had to contend with as social media has had a direct influence in their confidence during their most vulnerable formative years. Recent studies indicate that social media content caused 40% of teenagers to worry about their image.[4] Among teens with the highest social media use, 41% rated their overall mental health as poor or very poor.[5] Additionally, 60% of teens with high social media use and weak parental relationships reported poor or very poor mental health, and 22% of these teens expressed thoughts of suicide or self-harm.[6]

While social media has brought many positive outcomes to society, and I've personally leveraged it to build my brand and career, it can act as a double-edged sword, providing a platform for bad actors who can undermine the confidence we've painstakingly rebuilt since Imposter Syndrome first knocked on our heart's door. This is just one of many layered factors, alongside systemic barriers and other injustices women face both in and out of the workplace. In 2023, women earned only 83 cents for every dollar men earned[7] and global gender parity in the workplace is still 134 years away.[8] Believing in ourselves can feel more challenging today than ever before, given these disheartening societal factors. However, it's crucial to remember that confidence comes from both external and internal sources. While we can't control many of the outside factors, we can certainly focus on silencing Imposter Syndrome, disconnecting from outside influences, and trusting in our own abilities, even when others choose not to.

Microsoft's employees—including the She—certainly did, and the results were astronomically successful. The company has played a pivotal role in each of the four major digital revolutions, each marking a significant shift in how we engage with technology.

Personal Computing Revolution

The personal computing revolution of the 1970s and 1980s wasn't just about technology—it was about access, empowerment, and possibility. Microsoft's first mission, "A microcomputer on every desk and in every home running Microsoft software," set the stage for a world where computing belonged to everyone. In 1981, their bold move to acquire and transform QDOS into MS-DOS was a defining moment—proof that they could spot potential and reshape an industry. And in 1985, Windows 1.0 took things further, introducing a graphical interface that made computing more intuitive, opening doors for millions, and proving that technology isn't just about machines—it's about people.

Internet Revolution

The internet revolution of the 1990s changed everything—how we connect, share, and do business. Microsoft met the moment in

1995 with Windows 95 and Internet Explorer, weaving the internet into everyday computing and making it more accessible than ever. This era wasn't just about technology; it was about breaking barriers, fueling curiosity, and opening the world to new possibilities through the rise of the World Wide Web and the first web browsers. It was a time of bold moves, big shifts, and a whole new way of being connected.

Mobile + Cloud Computing Revolution

The mobile and cloud revolutions reshaped Microsoft's path, bringing a new era of innovation under Satya Nadella's leadership in 2014. The early 2000s saw mobile technology explode, with the iPhone's 2007 debut turning phones into powerful, always-connected computers. Microsoft took bold steps, acquiring Nokia's devices and launching Windows Phones, gaining invaluable insights into apps and ecosystems. In 2001, Xbox carved out a space in gaming, proving Microsoft could thrive beyond traditional computing. Then came the cloud revolution—by 2010, Azure redefined cloud computing, and in 2011, Office 365 transformed the workplace. By 2022, the Microsoft Cloud for Sustainability showed how technology could address global challenges, combining innovation with purpose.

AI Revolution

Currently, we are witnessing the AI revolution, which is progressing at an unprecedented pace and influencing all facets of our lives. In 2023, Microsoft reinforced its leadership in AI with the launch of Microsoft Copilot, an AI-powered productivity assistant designed to enhance how we work and create. As the company neared its 50th anniversary, it continued to evolve, introducing the Secure Future Initiative and Windows 12 with AI capabilities—further proof of its commitment to innovation and reinvention. Chapter 12 will take a deeper dive into what we now know as the Era of AI.

Sure, you might think it's easy to maintain confidence when everything seems to be going smoothly and you're riding a wave of success. But we all know that both in our personal lives and in the journey of every company, true success often comes hand in hand with failure. For Microsoft, defining moments of challenge offer us invaluable lessons on bouncing back and failing forward. Remember Windows Vista in 2007? Plagued by performance issues and compatibility problems, it faced a rocky reception. Back in 1995, Microsoft Bob aimed to simplify computing but was criticized for being too simplistic. Windows ME, launched in 2000, was notorious for instability, earning the nickname "Mistake Edition." The Microsoft Kin, a line of smartphones introduced in 2010, was discontinued within two months due to poor sales. The Microsoft Band, launched in 2014, faced a similar fate due to design flaws and lack of interest. And let's not forget Clippy, the Office Assistant from 1997, which was unsuccessful in helping users as originally envisioned, and was eventually removed (I personally loved it!). The Zune media player, released in 2006, couldn't compete with the iPod and was phased out by 2011, and Windows 8, released in 2012, was met with confusion and lukewarm reception due to its drastic interface changes.

Innovation demands vulnerability, resilience, and perseverance—qualities that we, the She, have embraced as our superpowers. But let's be real—showing up with courage isn't easy. It opens us up to criticism, competition, and those waiting for us to stumble. Women in and outside of tech often ask me if my fear of failure—or even success—ever stops me from putting myself out there and chasing big, bold ideas. My answer? I have a bigger fear: looking back one day and realizing I never dared to try.

At Microsoft, we don't just witness innovation—we live it. And in that process, we build confidence, not just through our own successes and failures, but by being in an environment that encourages us to grow, lead, and take risks. If half of confidence comes from external factors like support, past wins, and the belief of others, then Microsoft has been an extraordinary platform for the She to rise. Here's a personal story from Lan Ye, CVP Teams Engineering, on that very "She Confidence."

Teams Work Makes the Dream Work

I remember joining the Microsoft Teams project around its public launch in March 2017. At that time, Teams was primarily a persistent group chat app, inspired by the growing popularity of instant messaging in the business world. The idea was to create a central hub for collaboration, where people could share files, get things done, and communicate quickly and efficiently. We had Skype for Business, but it was built for an on-premises, client-server era. This architecture wasn't designed for the cloud, and we realized we needed a more cloud-native design to meet the evolving needs of our users.

The turning point came when we understood that our software distribution model was holding us back. We didn't control how companies updated their software, leading to a fragmented ecosystem with hundreds of different versions. At one point, Microsoft internally had more than 100 versions of the Skype for Business client in use. It took more than six months for a single line of code to reach 18% of our population, significantly hindering our ability to innovate and improve quality.

By 2019, we had achieved parity between Teams and Skype for Business and were ready to deprecate Skype for Business Online. This was a significant milestone, but an even bigger challenge loomed ahead. When COVID-19 hit in early 2020, the world suddenly needed a reliable, scalable solution for remote work and education.

Overnight, the demand for Teams skyrocketed. We went from onboarding individual companies to supporting entire countries' education systems. The scale of growth was unprecedented, and we had to rapidly enhance Teams' capabilities and performance to meet this new demand.

The pandemic forced the world to embrace digital transformation at an accelerated pace. Remote meetings and calls became the norm, and the importance of cloud-based solutions was more evident than ever. This period was intense but incredibly rewarding. We were not just building a product; we were helping the world stay connected during a global crisis.

Looking to the future with AI, I see immense opportunities for enhancing productivity and collaboration within Microsoft Teams. The focus is on leveraging AI to turn meetings and calls from black boxes into valuable sources of knowledge. Real-time transcription, audio-visual recognition, and other AI-driven features capture and analyze meeting content, improving collaboration and making information accessible for future reference. Years ago, I envisioned Teams enabling users to follow up on meetings quickly without attending every single one. Now, with Copilot in Teams and Recap, that's possible. It allows users to review key points and decisions made during meetings and define follow-ups efficiently, demonstrating the concrete value AI brings to meetings and driving enthusiasm for the future.

■ ■ ■

Lan's story illustrates the journey of embracing change and overcoming obstacles to foster innovation and resilience. Faced with the need for a cloud-native design, Lan and her team identified and addressed the hindrances in the software distribution model. This proactive approach, combined with a collaborative environment, allowed them to adapt quickly and support the massive surge in demand during the COVID-19 pandemic. Through perseverance and a clear vision, Teams evolved from a group chat app into a robust collaboration tool, leveraging AI to enhance productivity and communication. Lan's "She Confidence" was reinforced through continuous learning, teamwork, and the courage to innovate.

Your environment plays a crucial role in building confidence, just as much as your internal affirmations—it's 50% of the equation! While you can't always control every environment you're in, you do have the power and responsibility to remove yourself from toxic places that don't support your confidence. Yes, that means changing your company, your social circles, or any other environment that hinders your growth. It's not just about enduring; it's about thriving in spaces that nourish your self-belief and enable you to shine.

Do you remember the iconic "Maybe It's Maybelline" commercial that first aired in 1991 for Maybelline's Finish Matte line? That catchy jingle quickly became synonymous with the brand, emphasizing self-confidence and empowerment. "Maybe She's born with it. Maybe it's Maybelline" suggested that while natural beauty is inherent, Maybelline products could enhance and highlight it. The campaign aimed to help every woman feel confident and beautiful, regardless of whether their beauty was natural or makeup enhanced. Though my journey at Microsoft hasn't always been as smooth as a matte rose lipstick, I owe much of my career success to the company.

Maybe I was born with it, but maybe it's Microsoft: an environment where we endeavor a culture of learn-it-alls (better yet, learn-HER-alls—see Chapter 9 for more!), innovation, and inclusion.

A quick and fun parenthesis here to share in case you didn't know, Microsoft Teams has a Maybelline filter! The Maybelline Beauty App in Teams allows users to try out virtual makeup looks during video calls. Developed in collaboration with the Geena Davis Institute, the app offers 12 unique makeup styles that users can apply with a click. Powered by Modiface AI, it uses augmented reality technology to create a seamless virtual makeup experience. Maybe it's Maybelline AND Microsoft!

It is essential to recognize that the journey of the Microsoft She has not always been characterized by confidence. Indeed, her path has frequently been marred by anxiety, frustration, depression, hormonal imbalances, chronic illness, loneliness, sleeplessness, societal constraints, injustices, discrimination, and the barrenness of both children and ideas. From the moment she became aware of her identity as a She, she has been contending with factors beyond her control. This realization compelled her to write her own code to navigate these challenges and shape her own destiny.

Mary Snapp, VP Strategic Initiatives and also Microsoft's first lawyer, tells us how.

The Law of Confidence

Stepping into Microsoft as the only woman lawyer in the room, I felt like an outsider in more ways than one. I wasn't an engineer, I didn't speak their language, and I was dressed in a way that stood out in an office where formal attire was practically nonexistent. My job wasn't just about understanding the law—it was about earning credibility in a world that had never had to deal with someone like me before.

In those early days, I had to prove that I belonged. The engineers had never spoken to a lawyer before, and they weren't sure why they needed to start now. But I knew that to help the company, I had to understand the way they thought. I asked questions—endless questions. I listened. And then, something clicked. The way they described their decisions in coding wasn't so different from the Socratic method I had mastered in law school. Logic, reasoning, and problem-solving—these were the bridges between our two worlds. Once I realized that, my confidence grew.

The real breakthrough came when I noticed a shift in the room. Instead of sitting back with their arms crossed, they started leaning forward, grabbing grease pens, and sketching on the whiteboard. That was the moment I knew—I had earned their trust. I wasn't there to stop them; I was there to help them. And every time I saw that transition, I went home with a sense of triumph.

But confidence isn't just about knowledge—it's about resilience. Microsoft was going through challenging times, facing regulatory scrutiny that bred distrust on all sides. It was my job to act as a bridge, translating between engineers and government officials, finding common ground where there was none. There were heated moments, voices raised in frustration, but I learned when to stand my ground and when to be adaptable.

One particular moment stays with me. A senior developer, frustrated by new compliance demands, stood up and, with barely contained anger, challenged me. "You told us we wouldn't have to do this!" he said. I didn't waver. I met his frustration with calm resolve. "The landscape has changed," I told him. "You have to adapt." And over time, they learned that when I insisted on something, it truly mattered. Because I was flexible where I could be, they knew that when I took a firm stance, it was for a reason. That trust didn't come overnight. It was built conversation by conversation, decision by decision.

Through it all, my confidence as a woman in this space wasn't just about holding my own—it was about showing that I belonged, that my perspective was valuable, and that leadership comes in many forms. I have been at Microsoft for more than 36 years, through the highs and lows, through shifts in technology and leadership, through eras of expansion and introspection. And now, standing in the midst of the AI revolution, I feel the energy, the momentum, the excitement of yet another transformation. The journey has never been easy, but it has been worth it. Because confidence isn't about knowing all the answers—it's about knowing that you have the strength to find them.

■ ■ ■

In my experience, building self-confidence is a lot like writing code—you have to learn to command yourself. Think of it this way: you are both the programmer and the system in need of reprogramming. Just like in coding, the process starts with setting up the right environment, giving yourself the space to think and create, and then refining your inner dialogue until it runs smoothly. Confidence isn't something we're just born with—it's something we build, debug, and optimize along the way.

Years ago, when Imposter Syndrome had completely drained my confidence, I unknowingly started reprogramming myself. I created a three-step process—my own way of rewriting the code that was holding me back. What I didn't realize at the time was that I was developing a confidence programming language, one that worked not just for me, but for other women looking to stand tall in their own power.

Let's be real—this code won't make you perfect. In fact, we, the She, have learned to laugh in the face of perfectionism (see Chapter 7!). But what it *will* do is make you perfectly confident in your abilities. And that's the kind of code worth mastering.

The Confidence Algorithm

Know Yourself.

Like Yourself.

Love Yourself.

Know Yourself

I remember a time early in my career when I used to lie to myself pretty frequently. When people would ask if I worked out because

I'm naturally slim, I'd say yes. When they asked if I was a reader because I'm a writer, I'd also say yes. Yet, neither my calendar nor my wallet could confirm this. I probably hadn't picked up a book or gone to the gym in the past two months due to traveling or doing whatever else was keeping me busy. In reality, I wasn't a consistent reader or gym rat; I was someone who occasionally dabbled. At some point, I had to come to terms with my delusion and decide if I truly wanted to become a reader and a gym-goer, and why.

I realized that it was easier, perhaps lazier, or simply more soothing to convince myself that I was someone I wasn't, rather than take a deep, critical look at who I really was and embrace that person. It was incredibly scary for me to think about coming to terms with my true self and starting to like who I was, imperfections and all.

True confidence is built on a foundation of honesty and self-awareness. Only by facing and accepting our true selves can we begin to make meaningful changes and grow into the people we aspire to be.

Knowing yourself isn't just about self-awareness—it's about digging deep and truly understanding the layers that make you *you*. Your history, ancestry, personal story, genetics, personality traits, virtues, fears, motivations, culture, upbringing, environment, strengths, weaknesses, values, and passions all shape how you show up in the world. Confidence isn't something you can just flip on like a switch—it's built from the inside out.

Think of it this way: you can't write a solid piece of code without the right data. And you can't *code* confidence without first understanding the inputs that define who you are. When you take the time to gather that data, to really own your story, confidence becomes less about pretending and more about knowing.

The confident She of Microsoft—and the world—didn't just stumble into confidence. They put in the work. They dug deep, sifted through their stories, faced the hard truths, and calibrated their sense of self with clarity and intention. They didn't just ask, *Who am I?*—they asked, *Who do I want to become?* And just as importantly, they acknowledged their limitations.

True confidence comes from standing fully in your truth, unapologetically embracing your story, and maybe—even just a little—liking who you are in the process.

Like Yourself

Have you ever met a woman who doesn't like herself? I have—too many, in fact. These women are masters at spotting flaws, not just in themselves but in others. Operating from a place of insecurity, they often, unintentionally, pull other women into the same cycle of self-doubt. Their lack of self-acceptance isn't random—it's shaped by old wounds, past mistakes, and a reluctance to forgive, leaving them stuck in a loop where their self-worth gets buried beneath their perceived shortcomings.

I know this because I was one of them. My first *big girl* job out of college was brutal. I walked in bright-eyed and eager, ready to share my ideas and energy with the world. But my enthusiasm was met with resistance and ridicule from colleagues who saw me as too much—too eager, too young, too inexperienced. Slowly, my spark dimmed. Over time, I started blending in, playing it safe, muting the very things that once made me, *me.*

As my career progressed, I tried to reignite that spark, but the journey wasn't easy. The hardest part wasn't just recognizing my flaws—it was realizing how much space I had given them in my own head. I was so focused on what I lacked that I never took the time to appreciate what I brought to the table. And maybe that's why I had been dishonest with myself from the start—I didn't know how to embrace who I truly was.

Moving from simple *acceptance* to actually *liking* myself was not easy at all. It meant going deep, understanding where my insecurities came from, forgiving myself for past missteps, and refusing to let those moments define me. It was a slow, messy, necessary transformation—one that required real self-compassion and courage.

Confident women know that self-acceptance doesn't happen overnight. It's a process—one that demands patience, honesty, and a willingness to rewrite the narrative we tell ourselves. And when we do? That's where real confidence begins—the kind that isn't shaken by external noise but built from the inside out. That's the second layer in the algorithm of self-assurance, a foundation that allows us to move through life with authenticity, strength, and resilience.

Love Yourself

The final step in becoming a truly confident woman can feel downright excruciating—like debugging a system riddled with faulty code. And no wonder. Cultural, religious, and societal norms have conditioned women to equate selflessness with self-neglect, to see self-love as selfishness. Our deep capacity for compassion, community, and care is often exploited, leaving us feeling guilty for prioritizing ourselves, as if our own well-being is an afterthought. I know this struggle all too well—because, you guessed it, I've also lived it.

For years, I thought learning to *know* myself and then *like* myself would be enough. But it wasn't. It was just the beginning. True confidence required me to dig even deeper—to debug the outdated, harmful beliefs that had been running in the background for so long. I had to reprogram the way I saw myself, strip away the guilt, and learn to love myself in the purest and deepest way possible.

That's the hardest part of self-love—it forces us to confront the expectations we've internalized and rewrite them on our own terms.

It's uncomfortable, messy, and absolutely necessary. Because without this reprogramming, confidence remains surface-level. Real confidence—the kind that holds steady in the face of criticism, failure, or rejection—comes from an unshakable belief in our worth, no matter what the world tells us.

A truly confident woman carries herself with an undeniable sense of self-love. She knows exactly who she is, what she brings to the table, and she refuses to shrink for anyone. She dreams big, even when others try to make her feel small. She challenges the status quo—not out of arrogance, but because she *knows* she belongs in the room. Her perseverance isn't about endless energy or unbreakable resilience; it's about purpose. She gets tired. She gets weary. But she presses on, because she understands the importance of the trail she's blazing—for herself and for every woman who follows.

So, there you have it—the code of confidence is a multilayered, complex algorithm that you get to build, even if you have no prior coding experience. *Especially* if you don't. It's the programming that will enable you to debug external, and even internal, circumstances that have plagued your system for so long, crippling your true capability and authentic voice.

As Melinda Gates once said, "A woman with a voice is by definition a strong woman. But the search to find that voice can be remarkably difficult." Embrace the journey of searching, learning, liking and loving yourself, as difficult as it may be. It's a road less traveled, we know. But it's absolutely worth it. Take it from the She, and from Chapter 6—which will inspire you to tell your story, or someone else will!

Speaking of roads, did you know that 72.8% of women at Microsoft are in non-technical roles? So many women assume that working in tech means you *have* to be in a technical position, but that couldn't be further from the truth! The beauty of the tech industry—and especially Microsoft—is the incredible diversity of career journeys women have taken to get here, whether in technical or non-technical roles.

In Chapter 3, we'll dive into the stories of women who have built thriving careers in tech, sharing the strategies that helped them navigate and succeed. But first, come with me to the next chapter, where we'll uncover the fascinating, unexpected, and sometimes surprising paths that led women to Microsoft—and to the unique "rooms of the house" they now call home.

Chapter Recap

- A woman who steps up to shatter systemic barriers is a woman who proves that confidence can reshape industries and rewrite history.

- Mastering confidence isn't optional—it's essential. Learn how to build your personal brand with intention and clarity.

- Develop authentic confidence by cultivating self-awareness, practicing acceptance, and embracing self-love—despite societal expectations or personal doubts.

Embracing the Journey

Start practicing self-love today—right now. It doesn't have to be some grand, life-altering move. It could be as simple as skipping that extra sugary drink tomorrow. The truth is every small step matters. Every act of self-love, no matter how tiny, is a declaration to yourself that you are worthy.

Chapter 2

All Roads Lead to Microsoft

Empowering women in technology is not just about equality; it's about unlocking the full potential of our industry.
—Amy Hood, Chief Financial Officer at Microsoft

As of 2025, roughly 57,000 women are working at Microsoft—and that number keeps growing. It's truly inspiring to me to know that I have proximity to these many brilliant women, and the potential to learn from them, get to know them, befriend them, or even co-author a book with some of them. Hello, Miri!

While I don't know where all of us were, long before we found ourselves in the same tech bubble, I doubt any of us dreamed of working at Microsoft specifically. But I can picture us as little girls, with wide-open hearts and even wider imaginations, spinning dreams about the future. Some of us, including me, possibly spent hours dressing up as our favorite heroines, racing through the rooms of the house, embodying what the self-proclaimed Chief Troublemaker at Microsoft, Dona Sarkar, calls "and people." You know, the kind of kids who didn't want to choose between ballerina and astronaut, doctor and princess. Because honestly, what's the point of a white coat if you're not rocking it with a tutu?

And then adulting came along. We had to grow up, set aside our uninhibited imaginations, and step into the "real world." Suddenly, we were told to pick one path—and only one. There was no room for "and people" at university, or in life.

I still remember that overwhelming pressure to figure out my entire future, and to figure it out fast. The dreams I once held, vivid and brimming with possibility, began to feel like fleeting, romantic illusions. Choosing a field of study felt monumental, as though it alone could define the rest of my life. That decision, framed as final and unchangeable, cast a shadow over everything. And what a heavy load that was to bear at such a young age, with so much of life still waiting to unfold.

I often found myself wondering, *What if I hated the career path I chose? Was I even allowed to change my mind anywhere along the way?* And the hardest question of all: *Am I on the right path to do what I love, when I'm not even sure of who I am?*

Oh, how things have changed in just a few decades. Job trends show that reskilling is already a common thread in our careers,[1] with individuals needing to learn and grow multiple times as technology continues to weave itself into every corner of our lives.[2] Digital roles are expanding rapidly, shaping the future of work in ways we're just beginning to grasp.

This can only mean one thing: it's never too late to step into tech. In fact, there's never been a better time to lead it. You may not know this about my co-author Miri, but she's one of the remarkable women at Microsoft who reprogrammed herself to become an "and" person. She's a Senior Storyteller at Microsoft, and a twice-published author, and a renowned public speaker, and now the CEO of the world's first AI for women, Empressa.ai—a groundbreaking AI platform offering a secure and trustworthy space for women to connect, exchange insights, and support one another. You should really check it out!

I share this not only because I'm immensely proud of her, but because Miri embodies the very essence of the She in the industry. She often speaks passionately about the extraordinary opportunities women have today to not only join but lead in this new Era of AI.

Yet, despite the unprecedented possibilities opening up for women in tech, there's a sobering reality. While recent studies[3] show that generative AI technology is being adopted in the United States faster than the internet and personal computers ever were, studies also reveal a troubling disparity: men are adopting AI at significantly higher rates than women.[4] This mirrors historical patterns in technology adoption. If women don't close this gap, we risk exacerbating job disparities, skills gaps, and economic inequalities in the very near future.

Here's the truth: growth in tech isn't just about learning new tools or mastering new platforms. It's about weaving the wisdom of our past into the fresh challenges of the present, building a foundation for professional success.

Our paths aren't forged by a single factor—they're shaped by an intricate and remarkable blend of passion, talent, persistence, education, market opportunities, societal expectations, and those magical moments we like to call coincidences or destiny.

At Microsoft, this truth comes alive every day. The company welcomes an extraordinary mix of talented individuals, each bringing their unique stories, motivations, and aspirations. The journey into tech isn't linear or predictable. It's as diverse and dynamic as the people who dare to walk it.

Take Steph, for example. She found pure joy in learning to speak the language of machines. Or Débora who rewrote her destiny thread by thread, crafting a future she could finally call her own. There's Laiba, who joined the Microsoft Aspire University Hire program with her sights set on her dream company, and Jenia, who charted a bold course from the skies to the digital cloud. And then there's Kasia—a recruiter whose journey from candidate to career coach brings us full circle.

In the next few pages, we'll share their stories, and their *aha!* moments in tech—stories of courage, resilience, and curiosity to bring to light how these women didn't just land jobs in "Big Tech," they defied odds, chased passions, and seized every opportunity with both hands. Kasia will also leave you with invaluable insights and advice for anyone aspiring to carve out their own path in tech.

 WOW! I Can Make Machines Talk to Me! by Steph Burg, Principal Group Engineering Manager at Microsoft

It was another hot summer in the middle of Wisconsin, where technology felt more like something you'd see on TV than something that shaped real lives. In my community, a "real" job meant working on a farm with animals and grain, or on the assembly line at the auto manufacturer—tangible, practical work. Life was predictable, and nothing seemed destined to change.

When I got into college, I could have never imagined that my path would eventually lead me to Microsoft. Back then, my dream was to become a neonatal neurologist—a very specific kind of doctor focused on understanding and healing the newborn human brain. That dream consumed me as I studied biochemistry at the University of Wisconsin in Madison. Then life intervened in ways I couldn't have foreseen.

I discovered a program at my university for underrepresented minorities in computer science. It included extra discussion sessions led by peers, and I decided to join, mostly out of curiosity. A few months in, everything changed. I remember sitting in a dark basement computer lab writing my first "Hello World" program. In that moment, something clicked. I thought, Wow. I can make machines talk! It wasn't just cool—it was powerful. It opened a door I didn't even know existed. That was my first *aha!* moment, and it changed everything. I shifted my dreams and decided to pursue a dual major in biochemistry and computer science. It wasn't easy, but it was the right choice for me.

Graduating, though, was just the beginning. The real test came when I stepped into the working world. My first internship at Amazon was equal parts terrifying and exciting. I was assigned to explore an uncharted area and given full freedom to figure it out. For many, that would have been a dream. For me, it was intimidating. But I did it—and that success gave me a level of confidence I'd never had before.

That summer wasn't just about work. It was about finding myself. I changed my look—something that felt truer to who I was, even if it seemed "boyish" by my hometown's standards. I felt at ease in the big city and realized I could thrive there. For the first time, I felt like I'd found my place in the world.

The next year, I wanted to return to Amazon. But someone gave me advice that changed my trajectory: internships are an opportunity to explore. Reluctantly, I applied to Microsoft. When I interviewed, I was surprised. The people were warm, the project sounded fascinating, and the team felt like a real support system. I accepted the offer, and that summer changed everything.

Since then, I've never left Microsoft. I've grown with the company, from an intern to a Principal Manager, managing managers and leading teams. Along the way, I've also navigated life as a mother of four, learning to balance family and career while discovering my own superpowers. This journey has taught me something important: being an engineer isn't just about writing code. It's about the connections you make, the conversations you have, and the impact you create. For me, my strength lies in bringing people together—facilitating the right conversations with the right individuals to drive meaningful outcomes.

Looking back, I never could have predicted this path. But I've learned to embrace the unexpected, trust my instincts, and follow my dreams wherever they lead. So, if there's one thing I'd share with anyone out there wondering where their road might take them, it's this: don't be afraid to explore. All roads can lead to Microsoft—even if you didn't start in tech.

 Macchiatos, Macroeconomics, & Microsoft by Laiba A. Khan, Customer Success Account Manager

Amidst the aroma of roasted coffee, ruffles of freshly printed resumes, and restless nerves, hundreds of freshmen, including myself, lined up at our college career fair to shape our future.

Days leading up, students received guidance on every detail; from the firmness of our handshake to the conviction in our voice. To starch up our blazer, hem our pants with a perfect crease, and always keep a lint roller handy. We were accustomed to waiting two hours, just to gain two minutes of a recruiter's time.

But everything I knew about corporate recruiting atrophied during COVID. Limited jobs, blurred future, and human interactions were at an all-time low. I had the three most rigorous interviews of my career at my dream company, Microsoft, from home at my high school Ikea desk.

Throughout college, I enthusiastically, sometimes halfwittedly, kept applying on the Careers page, and collected a long list of "Not Selected" tags. But Microsoft didn't visit our university's business school back then, so I made the most of what I could act on. The persistence finally paid off when a recruiter reached out on LinkedIn.

My internships at EY and the IRS taught me about my strengths and weaknesses. I learned that I thoroughly enjoy engaging with people, having any two days be repetitive makes me gloomy, and I only need coffee when I'm siloed on an extensive Excel mission. I discovered that Sales is my strong suit, and V-lookups are not. I centered my search around relationship building and started my first ever full-time position as a Customer Success Account Manager (CSAM).

Microsoft sets up their university recruits annually into a two-year long program called Aspire. Our onboarding was entirely virtual, but we didn't realize how dependable our friendships would be for years to come.

The CSAM role is constantly evolving. Crafting relationships is a beautiful but delicate process, especially when it's with customers who are entrusting you with multi-million-dollar portfolios. When you are 22, you believe that you, alone, can do everything under the sun. However, a client-facing professional should never operate in isolation. Forming relationships with your Account Executives, Incident Managers, and Product Specialists is key. I found my might in breaking down technical jargon and translating it into comprehendible concepts. After all, we can only expect clients to trust us with their time and financial investment when they understand what we are selling to them.

One year in, I helped lead the "Aspire Reverse Mentorship Program." We flipped conventional mentorship and allowed young professionals (mentees) to educate their managers (mentors) on how they want to be guided, managed, and led. I pursued executive sponsorship to establish the project's credibility and create a lasting impact. With utmost optimism, I precisely wrote my proposal and reached out to Satya Nadella, CEO of Microsoft, along with every single executive vice president. Jean-Philippe Courtois, EVP of National Partnerships, graciously accepted to watch and provide his feedback on our final two presentations. The experience confirmed my confidence in always pushing the highest limit possible and never rejecting myself from opportunities. It's critical to incorporate fun extracurriculars and career development activities that can serve as a creative outlet. You must keep stirring the pot, so you don't get stuck and burn out.

When I was 10 years old, hopping around the International Departures area at Karachi Airport, I didn't comprehend what "immigrating" to the United States meant. But I knew that I had to make my family's bold move count. In my 3.5 years at Microsoft, every win and challenge has been accompanied by impactful mentors and teachable moments. With every blocker—be it young age that can be perceived for inexperience, my Pakistani heritage that's still underrepresented in big tech, or being a woman—comes the grand responsibility of developing intellectual security, and leveling the playing field for ourselves, our peers, and our future generation.

Stitching a New Future by Débora Di Piano, Digital Native Account Executive

I grew up in a modest home shaped by the industrious spirit of the women in my life—my grandmother and mother. They worked tirelessly, crafting uniforms for organizations to provide for our family. From a young age, I absorbed their strong work ethic and the desire to create a different path for myself. I loved them deeply but knew I wanted more than to follow in their footsteps.

At 15, I made a decision that would change my life. My inspiration came from a friend I knew who was studying electronics with an aviation focus. His passion was contagious; I soaked up his enthusiasm as he talked about planes and aircrafts. That's when I realized I wanted to pursue technology—not sew uniforms.

It wasn't an easy decision. My family couldn't afford the tuition for the technical school I dreamed of attending, but I was determined. I took on part-time work with my mother, spending hours after school sewing uniforms to pay for my education. It was exhausting, but I knew it was my key to a different life.

My interest in technology blossomed into a love for programming and electronics. Still, my first encounter with Microsoft felt like a twist of fate. At the age of 19, I attended an interview, shortly after graduating in Electronics, for a Java developer position, but the interviewer suggested I might be better suited for a role as an Application Lifecycle Management (ALM) consultant. I didn't fully understand what the role entailed, but I said yes, trusting that I could learn.

When I arrived at the address the recruiter gave me—*Bouchard 710 in Buenos Aires*—I thought perhaps I became lost. A man on the street pointed to a building with a massive Microsoft logo, and it hit me: I would be working for Microsoft!

That realization brought a wave of emotions—excitement mixed with a deep sense of self-doubt. *Could I do this? Was I good enough?* Imposter Syndrome hit hard. I spent countless nights crying, studying, and convincing myself that I could learn.

My father was my rock during that time. Every morning, he'd take the train with me to work, patiently listening as I practiced my presentations and talked through technical concepts. He didn't understand the technology, but his presence gave me the strength I needed to push forward. Those first months were tough, but they shaped me. My manager pushed me hard but also saw my potential. Slowly, I built confidence, immersing myself in learning, dedicating extra hours, and proving to myself that I belonged.

A pivotal moment came when I began working directly on customer projects. Applying my knowledge in real-world scenarios showed me the tangible impact of my work, and for the first time, I truly felt like I belonged at Microsoft. My transition to a full-time employee solidified that sense of belonging. Eventually, I decided to explore opportunities outside Microsoft. But as they say, all roads lead [back] to Microsoft. When Satya Nadella's leadership brought a cultural refresh to the company, I was inspired to return.

At the time, I was transitioning to Spain and hesitant to change jobs again. But Microsoft's new culture drew me in. After a smooth interview process, I was thrilled to receive an offer—only to discover shortly after that I was pregnant. I emailed human resources to explain that I couldn't take the position. The hiring manager reached out personally, telling me, "We don't hire people for the short term; we hire for the long term. If you still want to be part of my team, you're welcome—whenever you're ready." That unwavering support solidified my decision to rejoin Microsoft, where I've been ever since.

Today, I look back at my journey with pride. Having a specific vision played a big role in getting me here. I've always pictured my future self—successful, confident, and surrounded by a supportive network. That vision has evolved over the years. It's no longer just about career success; it's about creating a balanced life where I can thrive both professionally and personally, being present for my family while achieving my goals.

Microsoft isn't just a company to me—it's a part of my story, a place where I've grown, stumbled, and succeeded. And it all started with a dream, a lot of sewing, and the belief that I could stitch up a different path for myself.

Forecast: Clear Skies with a Digital Cloud, by Jenia Fulton, Logistics Technician

Growing up in Panama, a small yet globally connected country known for the Panama Canal, I always had vivid dreams about the future. Like many kids, I imagined myself as a singer or a princess, but as I grew up, I took a more practical path and decided to study logistics and multimodal transport—a natural fit given Panama's position as a global hub.

Yet, one childhood dream remained constant: I wanted to explore the world. This desire was non-negotiable, and it led me to apply for a flight attendant position with Qatar Airways. The selection process was intense—20 candidates chosen from 500—but with each stage I passed, my confidence grew. Even so, after months of waiting without news, I accepted a logistics job at LG Electronics in Panama. Then, out of the blue, Qatar Airways contacted me. They wanted my final test results to begin the visa process.

The choice wasn't easy. My new job at LG offered growth opportunities, but Qatar Airways promised a tax-free salary three times higher and the chance to fulfill my dream of traveling. My boss at LG encouraged me to seize the opportunity while I was young, and with my family's support, I made the leap to Qatar.

Moving to Qatar was a culture shock. I had never traveled outside Panama before and had to adapt to an entirely new environment. But it was worth it—I was finally living my dream. As a flight attendant, I visited countless countries, experienced different cultures, and grew in ways I never imagined.

One thing became clear quickly: my English needed improvement. In Panama, where Spanish is the primary language, English hadn't been a priority. But in the global environment of Qatar Airways, I had to adapt fast to communicate effectively with colleagues and passengers from around the world. I gained confidence and was eventually promoted to business class.

After five years of constant travel and irregular hours, however, the physical and mental toll began to weigh on me. The COVID-19 pandemic forced me to pause and reflect. What started as a planned two-year adventure had turned into five years, and I realized it was time to return to my original field: logistics. Determined to make a change, I began applying for jobs and came across an opportunity at Microsoft as a logistics technician in a data center. Despite not having a tech background, I decided to apply. The interview process focused on my interpersonal skills and ability to handle challenges—areas where my experience as a flight attendant shone.

The interviewers saw my potential, and I was offered the job. Starting at Microsoft was both exciting and nerve-wracking. I had to quickly learn about data center operations, but my eagerness to learn helped me complete the onboarding process in just one month. I even surprised myself!

One of my *aha!* moments came when my onboarding partner went on vacation, leaving me to manage the site alone. It was a test of everything I had learned, and I realized I was capable of handling the responsibility. Looking back, I see how much my time as a flight attendant prepared me for this role. Skills I once underestimated proved invaluable:

- **Problem-Solving:** Handling in-flight emergencies taught me to think on my feet, a skill I now use to troubleshoot technical issues.
- **Teamwork:** Collaborating with a diverse crew gave me the ability to work effectively with colleagues from various backgrounds.
- **Multitasking:** Managing passenger needs while ensuring safety protocols honed my ability to juggle multiple priorities.
- **Time Management:** In the fast-paced airline world, every minute matters—a skill that helps me meet deadlines in my current role.
- **Interpersonal Skills:** Interacting with passengers improved my communication, crucial for collaboration in the tech world.
- **Resilience:** The demanding nature of the job built a resilience that helps me stay calm under pressure today.

One moment that stands out is a casual lunch with my manager. She explained why I was chosen for the role: "I was curious about your background." That curiosity reflects Microsoft's culture, where diverse experiences are celebrated. Since joining Microsoft, I've regained confidence in my abilities and discovered a passion for learning. My past as a flight attendant—often dismissed as superficial by some—gave me a unique perspective and skill set that continues to serve me well.

My story is a reminder that we should never underestimate our potential or let others define our worth. Whether in the skies or at a data center, I've learned that growth and success come from embracing change and believing in ourselves. Whatever my next dream may be, I know I'm ready to make it happen.

From Meat to Microsoft by Kasia Stańczak, Senior Technical Recruiter

Born and raised in Poland, I initially pursued studies in foreign trade and cultural studies, never imagining a future in the technology industry. With no technical background and no family ties to computer science, I didn't think a career in tech was possible. Yet, here I am—a recruiter at Microsoft.

As the first in my family to attend university, my academic journey took me from Poland to Germany, where I encountered different perspectives and new challenges. It was a significant achievement for both me and my family, who supported me despite the financial strain. Their encouragement gave me strength, reminding me that no matter where life took me, I would always have a home to return to.

After completing my studies, I started working in recruitment—but in the meat industry. Yes, you read that right: the meat industry! Back then, recruitment was a vastly different process. Without LinkedIn or digital tools, the phone was my best friend as I searched for candidates to fill positions in meat factories. That experience, while unconventional, taught me the fundamentals of recruitment and gave me confidence that I was good at what I did.

The turning point for me came when a friend transitioned to a completely new role at Microsoft. Watching her, I realized that one job doesn't have to define your career forever. This was an eye-opener for me, as I had grown up in a household where lifelong careers were the norm—my father as a police officer and my mother as a court clerk. While those career paths were admirable, seeing new possibilities felt like opening a window to a wider world.

When a friend suggested I apply for a recruitment role at Microsoft, I was ready to take the leap. The process was rigorous—eight interviews!—but my adaptability and determination carried me through. I joined Microsoft in 2014, just as Satya Nadella was taking the reins and reshaping the company's culture.

The timing couldn't have been better. Microsoft was transforming, with a focus on technical roles and a shift from hiring for experience alone to hiring for potential. Satya introduced the concept of a growth mindset, and it became central to how we approached recruitment.

Today, as a recruiter specializing in technical roles, I thrive in this ever-evolving landscape. The recruitment process at Microsoft is highly standardized to ensure fairness and inclusivity. For engineering roles, the process includes five main stages:

1. **Initial Screening with a Recruiter:** A preliminary conversation to assess background, skills, and interest in the role.
2. **Coding Interview:** Candidates solve a coding problem in real time, showcasing both their technical skills and problem-solving approach.
3. **Software Design Interview:** This involves designing a software solution, assessing the candidate's ability to architect systems.

4. **System Design Interview:** Candidates tackle complex system architecture and scalability challenges.
5. **Behavioral Interview (Work Culture Fit):** This stage explores the candidate's growth mindset, commitment to diversity and inclusion, and alignment with Microsoft's values.

What makes Microsoft's recruitment process unique is its alignment with our core values of respect, integrity, and accountability. These principles guide every hiring decision, ensuring we seek candidates who not only excel technically but also embody a commitment to diversity, collaboration, and ethical behavior.

Our focus on diversity and inclusion extends beyond gender or cultural background to encompass neurodiversity and other aspects of individuality. For example, we provide accommodations such as extra time for candidates with dyslexia or written responses for those who stutter, ensuring fairness for everyone.

As a recruiter and a parent of a 4-year-old, I deeply appreciate Microsoft's emphasis on work-life balance. Flexibility isn't just a benefit—it's a core part of our culture, from accommodating candidates' needs during interviews to supporting employees as they navigate family responsibilities.

I also love helping candidates navigate the recruitment process, and I want to share a few tips to help you succeed:

Before You Apply

- **Understand the Job Description:** Focus on the required qualifications; the preferred ones are a bonus.
- **Apply Even If You Don't Meet All Criteria:** Many candidates, especially women, hesitate to apply unless they meet every requirement. Take the chance!

- **Customize Your Resume:** Tailor it to the job description, highlighting relevant skills.
- **Leverage LinkedIn:** Optimize your profile and connect with recruiters. Join relevant groups and stay active.
- **Reach Out to People:** Don't hesitate to connect with people at Microsoft, including recruiters, to learn more about roles you're interested in and to introduce yourself. Additionally, reach out to professionals for guidance—mentors at Microsoft can offer valuable advice and help you prepare for opportunities.

During the Interview

- **Prepare Thoroughly:** Practice coding problems or system design questions. Showcase your work on GitHub and conduct mock interviews.
- **Be Honest About Your Needs:** If you require accommodations, communicate them early.
- **Demonstrate a Growth Mindset:** Share examples of how you've learned from mistakes and embraced challenges.
- **Highlight Collaboration Skills:** Showcase your ability to work well in teams and communicate effectively.
- **Drive for Results:** Discuss past projects where you made a significant impact.

Working at Microsoft has been transformative. It's not just a job—it's a place where curiosity, diversity, and potential are celebrated. My journey from the meat industry to tech is proof that with the right mindset and determination, you can carve a path that aligns with your dreams.

■ ■ ■

To anyone considering a role at Microsoft, here's what I want to say: take the leap. You might just surprise yourself. Because here's the truth: we're all women, but we can also be "and" women in tech. If you're ready to explore what's next, flip the page. Let's dive into the many rooms of the tech house—you might just find the one that feels like home.

> **Chapter Recap**
>
> - The path to a career in tech isn't a straight line—it's as unique as the women who walk it. Women at Microsoft have found success by embracing change, taking risks, and trusting their ability to learn and adapt. Your path is yours to shape.
>
> - AI is revolutionizing industries, but there's still a gender gap in who's leading the charge. We need more women stepping into AI spaces, driving innovation, and making sure inclusivity isn't an afterthought—it's a priority.
>
> - Embrace being an "and" person—You don't have to fit into one box. You can be analytical *and* creative; technical *and* strategic. The most fulfilling careers come from blending your passions and strengths into something uniquely *you*.

> **Embracing the Journey**
>
> Your journey into tech—or any dream career—doesn't have to start early, follow a straight line, or look like anyone else's. Whether you're pivoting from a completely different field or rediscovering a passion you put on the back burner, every step you've taken adds value to your story.

Chapter 3
Dream House

Welcome to my Dreamhouse! It's pink, it's fabulous, and it's filled with endless possibilities!

—Barbie

I remember the first time the Barbie Dreamhouse commercial flickered onto our small, manually tuned family television in Caracas, Venezuela. The vivid shades of pink and blue leapt off the screen, breaking the monotony of my day. As the ad unfolded, I was instantly transported into a magic world. Room by room, the camera lingered on every perfect detail: the chic living room with plush furniture, the glamorous bedroom with a canopied bed, and those sun-soaked balconies where Barbie—let's be honest, *me* in this fantasy—could sip tea and watch the sunset with her friends.

Back then, the Dreamhouse cost about $100,[1] which for my family might as well have been a million. In today's economy, experts estimate[2] that Barbie's Dreamhouse, if real, would cost a staggering $10 million. And that why it's called a dream house!

Growing up, many of us dreamed of having a home—whether it was Barbie's or one we imagined for ourselves. For women especially, the idea of home—not just a house—is often woven into our vision of the future. A home is more than walls and furniture; it's something we create, a reflection of who we are, something intangible that shapes the tangible world around us.

Interestingly, at Microsoft, they use the phrase "rooms of the house" to describe the various business functions that support the technology they create. These diagrams map out product cycles, with each "room" representing a step in the road map. But for you, our reader, let's put aside the usual charts and take a more imaginative approach. Let's step into the house—not as a framework but as a living, breathing metaphor. Let's bring each room—the women and their stories—to life, and explore how, just as in real life, the She has strived to turn this tech house into a tech home.

Imagine stepping into a house where every room tells a story—a story of purpose, connection, and how everything works together. At first glance, you see the outside—the walls, the roof, the façade. It's easy to assume it's all straightforward, the way people often think of the people behind the technology as just programmers or system administrators. But when you step through the front door, a deeper truth unfolds: this house, like tech, is alive with complexity and interconnection. Every room matters. Every space has a role to play. And every woman has a place to be and make her own.

We begin outside, on the front porch—the space where the organization opens itself to the world. This is where marketing, branding, public relations, and communications teams craft the first impression, sharing stories, values, and accomplishments. It's a space that reflects the house's identity and sets the tone for everything that happens inside.

Having spent most of my career on this "porch" myself, I can tell you it's more than just exciting—it's a dynamic space brimming with opportunities to create, innovate, and inspire. This is where we think of new ways to connect with our customers, to build trust, and to make them love the brand with words and visual elements. I remember listing my job title on LinkedIn as "Storyteller" at Microsoft more than six years ago. Within days, I received dozens of messages from curious colleagues asking, "What is that role? How did you get it?" Back then, storytelling as a business function was novel. Today, more companies are embracing it, recognizing that storytelling is not just about communication but about connection. This evolution mirrors the nature of the porch itself—a place of constant growth and new beginnings. Just like the flowers that bloom along the edges throughout the seasons, this space continues to evolve throughout the company's market seasons, offering new ways to bring the mission to life and invite others into the story of what we do.

Step inside, and you find yourself in the living room, the heart of connection. This is where relationships flourish, representing sales and customer success teams. Here, customers are welcomed, their needs are understood, and trust is built. It's a warm and lively space where meaningful interactions happen, setting the stage for lasting partnerships. Yet, as with any home, there are times when the furniture needs rearranging—not necessarily for the customer, but for the She, in order for her to make herself comfortable and excel at her role. And this exactly what Weronika Skowera, Customer Success Account Manager, did.

The Art of Tech Homemaking

When I first joined Microsoft, I had no technical background at all. Everything I learned about the world of IT and technology, I learned on the job. Over the years, I've held various business roles within the organization, but one of the most transformative ones was my time as a Customer Success Manager for Modern Workplace. My focus was on helping and supporting the biggest Microsoft customers in adopting Microsoft Teams.

I started this role just before the COVID-19 pandemic hit. My first month was spent directly at a client's office, working on a project to support migration and implementation of Teams for an organization with nearly 7,000 employees in the media industry. Imagine the client's surprise when a young woman with no prior technical experience showed up to lead such a significant and crucial migration project. It was a trial by fire, and I owe a lot to my manager for throwing me into the deep end.

I remember walking into the client's office on my first day, feeling a mix of excitement and sheer terror. The office buzzed with activity, and I could sense the skepticism in the air. Who was this young non-technical lady from Microsoft, and what did she know about managing such a massive migration project? Little did they know, I was asking myself the same question.

The first week was all about understanding the client's needs and the existing infrastructure. I spent hours in meetings, listening, taking notes, and asking questions. My lack of technical background turned out to be an advantage. I approached problems from a different perspective, often finding creative solutions that more experienced tech professionals might overlook.

As a woman in tech at that time, I faced my fair share of skepticism and doubt from other people. There were times when I felt the weight of prejudice, with some customer employees subtly implying that I wouldn't be able to make a significant impact. I vividly remember one meeting where a man looked me straight in the eye and said, "You won't succeed here." Instead of letting his words bring me down, I used them as fuel to prove him wrong. That man's words, meant to undermine me, ended up being a catalyst for my growth. They reminded me of the importance of resilience and self-belief. And as I continued to succeed, I realized that my journey wasn't just about proving others wrong—it was about proving to myself that I could overcome any obstacle. I threw myself into the project with even more determination. Every challenge became an opportunity to demonstrate my capabilities.

One of the biggest challenges was gaining the trust of the IT team. They were seasoned professionals, and here I was, a newcomer with no technical experience. I focused on building relationships, showing them that I was there to support and collaborate, not to dictate. Slowly but surely, they began to see the value I brought to the table.

Working primarily with the IT department, I also supported business users through this change. It wasn't my technical expertise that mattered most, but my ability to communicate effectively, approach problems creatively, and connect the right people within Microsoft to ensure success. The project concluded with great success, as we uncovered numerous scenarios for using Teams, and adoption rates soared.

The pandemic hit just as we were gaining momentum. Suddenly, the need for a robust communication and collaboration platform became even more critical. The pressure was on, but so was the opportunity to make a real impact. We worked around the clock, navigating the complexities of remote work and ensuring that the transition to Teams was as smooth as possible.

One of the most rewarding moments was when the customer held a virtual town hall meeting using Teams. Seeing thousands of employees seamlessly connect and engage was a testament to our hard work. The feedback was overwhelmingly positive, and adoption rates skyrocketed.

In the end, I didn't just succeed; I thrived at this project. I hope this story inspires other women in tech to keep pushing forward, no matter what challenges they face. We all have the power to make a difference, and sometimes, the greatest motivation comes from those who doubt us the most.

■ ■ ■

If Weronika's story doesn't wrap around your heart like a cozy throw in the living room, I don't know what will! Weronika has truly made a home for herself at Microsoft. She intuitively understood how to shape herself and her environment so that both she and her internal and external customers could feel completely at ease—like they truly belong.

At Microsoft, this is what the company calls "brand love." Simply put, it means creating a connection so strong that employees and customers can confidently say, "Microsoft is for people like me," and "I trust Microsoft." It's about transforming a house into a home.

When it comes to trust and connection, beyond the living area, the kitchen often stands out as the heart of the home—bustling with activity and vibrant with life. According to the U.S. Bureau of Labor Statistics, Americans spend an average of 37 minutes per day in the kitchen. Over a lifetime, that's nearly 800,000 minutes! And there's a good reason for it. Experts agree that shared activities, like cooking, play a significant role in building trust and strengthening bonds. Anthropological studies highlight the importance of communal meals in fostering trust and cohesion across cultures,[3] while sociological research emphasizes how daily rituals of cooking and eating together build social ties and trust within communities.[4]

Growing up in a family that made it a point to eat dinner together—and passing that tradition on to my children—I can wholeheartedly confirm that food preparation, sharing, and dining together are powerful trust-building experiences.

At Microsoft, the kitchen is where the magic happens—a space where creativity, skill, and innovation converge to create something truly extraordinary. Picture the brilliant product teams as master chefs, working with the finest ingredients to perfect recipes that delight and inspire. For more than 50 years, these chefs have been refining timeless classics while fearlessly experimenting with bold, new flavors. These recipes—the product innovations—are treasures that reflect not only the company's legacy but also its unwavering commitment to excellence.

But even the most inspired dishes need a taste test, a little feedback, to ensure they're as extraordinary as they can be. That's where teams like CAPE (Customer and Partner Ecosystem) come in. They're the trusted taste testers and collaborators, partnering with the developers to refine and elevate every creation to meet the highest standards of quality and delight.

One of these incredible collaborators is my co-author, Izabela Duiwe, lovingly known as Izzy. As a Senior Customer Experience Program Manager and a vital part of the CAPE team, Izzy works at the forefront of M365 Copilot technology. Her work explores new extensibility concepts with strategic customers across Central and Eastern Europe, the Middle East, and Africa. For those new to the concept, Copilot Extensibility enables customers to seamlessly integrate their organizational data, processes, and apps into Copilot's AI experience. It's like serving up a perfectly tailored meal—crafted to meet each customer's unique needs and tastes.

Izzy's passion for customer obsession and leveraging technology shines through in her work. As she puts it: "Our focus on customer needs and leveraging technology is key. It's so rewarding to bring our AI concepts to customers early on, validate them, and then take those insights back to improve the product. I love being part of an incubation, globally distributed team—it gives us a comprehensive view of challenges and opportunities across the world. Copilot Extensibility with agents is the future! Customers have so much data and so many systems to manage and simplifying that into one AI-driven user experience is not just powerful—it's transformational. This truly fulfills our vision of Copilot as UI for AI."

Izzy and her team ensure that the Microsoft recipes are not only delicious but also meet the diverse needs of its customers, bringing new flavors and possibilities to the table. Her work exemplifies how the She turns a house into a home, one dish at a time.

Off the kitchen is the pantry, where supplies are stored and organized. This room represents procurement and supply chain functions, ensuring the organization has what it needs—from raw materials to essential tools—to operate efficiently.

The study or home office represents a space of focus and planning—the intellectual hub of the house. This is where the finance and strategy teams work, analyzing data, forecasting growth, and determining which opportunities are worth pursuing. It's a place where curiosity and precision come together to shape the future. Beyond their analytical roles, the finance team members also play a hands-on part in bringing the technology to customers, acting as "customer zero" to test and refine solutions before they're released to the world. Gabriella Joo, Group Finance Manager, takes us on a tour of the home office room.

The Customer Zero Math

In finance, we may not be the first to dive into untested waters—our work requires stability and precision. But we are often the first testers of Microsoft's products, which puts us ahead of other finance teams in the industry. It's not about pressure; it's about opportunity.

I never planned or intended to work at Microsoft, but it has turned into a very rewarding journey. The company offers incredible opportunities, and I genuinely love the culture. For the past 10 years, I've been part of Microsoft Finance, working in Corporate Financial Planning and Analysis (FP&A). My journey began in the fast-moving consumer goods industry (FMCG), where I worked in finance after earning my degree in economics. I wasn't actively searching for a new job, but I left the door open. When a headhunter approached me with an opportunity at Microsoft, I was intrigued. As a finance professional who frequently used Excel, the idea of working for the company that created such an essential tool felt exciting and perfectly fitting.

I started in Microsoft's consumer division, which wasn't vastly different from my experience in FMCG. This made my transition into the tech industry smooth and manageable. I was both excited and curious to join the IT world, and despite not having a technical background, I felt at home in my new role. Classic finance principles applied here, too—after all, the same customer buying shampoo and ice cream might also buy Office software or an Xbox. My finance knowledge was highly valued, and I quickly realized I could make meaningful contributions to the business.

This consumer-focused entry point allowed me to familiarize myself with Microsoft's culture and operations, which further deepened my confidence. Over time, I recognized the diversity within Microsoft's finance sector and started exploring new opportunities. After a few years in the consumer division, I was certain I wanted to stay at Microsoft.

When I transitioned to the enterprise segment, I encountered a steeper learning curve, as this area was much more nuanced, particularly with Microsoft's cloud journey. I realized that starting my career in enterprise would have been a much more challenging experience, so I appreciated the foundation I built in the consumer space. This transition was made easier through an internal role swap, allowing me to remain within the Hungarian subsidiary while gaining a broader perspective.

Over time, I gained enough confidence to contribute on multiple levels. While my core responsibilities remained my primary focus, I never felt constrained by rigid job descriptions or boundaries. My passion for tools and reporting led me to become a "super user" of a planning tool. When I'm passionate about something, I dive in wholeheartedly, and this enthusiasm eventually earned me a project manager role for the tool at the corporate level. This opened the door for me to move to Microsoft's corporate headquarters in the United States.

In my current role as part of the corporate FP&A team, I focus on annual planning, particularly the field aspect. My role involves providing tools, guidelines, and playbooks that empower field finance teams to prepare for planning. This work is critical in ensuring accurate assumptions and baselines, which directly impact the company's financial health and strategic direction.

Microsoft has given me the platform to grow, challenge myself, and make meaningful contributions—all while reinforcing my belief in the value of culture, innovation, and teamwork.

■ ■ ■

As you can see, there are a multitude of opportunities to move around just in one room of the house! Down the hall, we find the guest room, a welcoming space for new arrivals. This room reflects the role of human resources, who ensure that employees feel valued, onboarded, and supported throughout their journey. HR also nurtures the internal "family," fostering collaboration, well-being, and a sense of belonging. Melissa Luongo, HR Director Central Europe, welcomes us to the guest room.

The "Human" in Human Resources

As an HR leader it is my job to support managers and leaders to attract and develop IT talents and to build and drive effective organizational changes aligned to company strategy. I also ensure that statutory governance is met in countries where we employ people and support each site to be a best place to work. I love that my role has an important seat at the table, as people are such an integral part of any technology business and bringing to life a People Plan is energizing. Our HR company mission is to "Be the most thriving, digitally-enabled, and diverse company on the planet, helping people achieve more" and I feel energized to be part of this mission/goal. If I think of the value I bring as a non-technical leader, I would say that I bring human centricity to everything that I do. Of course, in the field of "human" resources you would think that is a given, yet you have to role model it and also drive it within the culture of the organization you support. I have supported many diverse leadership teams over my tenure and ensuring that we have managers who model, coach, and care (an internal goal and metric for people managers) is so important. When we look for talent, yes, we want to ensure that they have the technical or sales skills needed to be successful in their role, but it is just as important that they have the attributes and behaviors that can be a cultural fit for the team and company. Holding culture as a high bar is something that I am proud of in my work.

■ ■ ■

Adjacent to the guest room is the family room—a bright, welcoming space where everyone comes together. This room symbolizes diversity, equity, and inclusion (DEI) efforts, ensuring that every voice is heard, valued, and empowered. It's where a sense of belonging and community is cultivated, turning the house into a home for everyone. As Lindsay-Rae McIntyre, Chief Diversity Officer and Corporate Vice President of Talent and Learning at Microsoft, affirms,[5,6] "We continue to believe it's the business of Microsoft to be diverse and inclusive so we can build products, services, and a workforce that empowers the world."

In the next chapter, we will explore the impact of DEI in the tech industry for She. But for now, follow me to the bedrooms. The quiet and private places that symbolize the behind-the-scenes work of chief of staffs and operations teams. These roles ensure the organization's rhythm of business, stability, security, and adherence to regulations. They're not always visible, but they provide the safety and trust that allow the rest of the house to thrive. Here to invite us into one of those bedrooms is Na-Young Choi, Chief of Staff.

La Touche de NaY

Being a Chief of Staff is about striking a fine balance between managing the present and envisioning the future. This role sharpens essential skills such as leadership, communication, adaptability, strategic decision-making, and coaching. It's a unique challenge that has strengthened me both professionally and personally.

I graduated in Industrial Engineering, where part of my curriculum involved learning to code in various languages. This sparked my interest in the IT world, though I knew early on I wouldn't become a developer or a traditional IT engineer. It was the late 1990s, and the internet was booming, opening up possibilities I couldn't ignore. Strangely, I could spend hours immersed in web development projects, unlike the thermodynamics assignments I procrastinated on. It took me some time to realize that my future was in IT, but once I did, it set the course for my career.

Nineteen years ago, fresh out of university, I joined Microsoft as part of the MACH program (Microsoft Academy for College Hires). With my engineering background, I applied to the MACH Technical track. During my assessment, the HR person noted, "You're probably the least technical candidate here today." They weren't wrong. But I got the job and started two months later as a SharePoint Technical Pre-Sales Engineer—a role I knew nothing about in a field I wasn't technically qualified for. Did I benefit from being a woman in tech? Perhaps. Or maybe Microsoft saw potential in me.

At the time, I joined a team of senior male experts, each with more than a decade of consulting experience. It was the first time the pre-sales team in France had hired a junior—and a woman. While the onboarding process prepared me with training and a ramp-up phase, I knew I couldn't compete with my colleagues' years of expertise. Instead, I leaned into my differences. I decided to focus on three things:

1. Low-code/no-code solutions (yes, they existed even then).
2. Creating compelling end-user scenarios that brought technical concepts to life.
3. Customizing demos with a tailored look and feel, helping customers see their brand reflected in the solution.

Ironically, being the least technical person on the team became my greatest strength. My learning curve mirrored that of the customer, enabling me to simplify complex concepts and focus on practical, relatable outcomes. Early in my career, I discovered the value of adapting, learning smartly, and bringing my own unique contributions to the table. This mindset became part of what I now call the "NaY's touch."

During my first year in the MACH Program, I earned my MCSE (Microsoft Certified System Engineer) certification, learning about infrastructure, networking, and identity management. Though I wasn't destined to be a technical expert, this knowledge proved invaluable. It helped me build environments for hands-on customer experiences and eventually led to the creation of the Customer Immersion Center—a best practice from France that was later adopted globally.

Over time, I realized how much I loved learning on the job. I've never been to a formal sales school, studied marketing, or pursued an MBA, but Microsoft became my 19-year (and counting) MBA. I've had the opportunity to work in sales, marketing, customer success, strategy, and people management across France, Europe, and globally.

Today, I proudly serve as Chief of Staff to Microsoft France's CVP—the first woman to hold the CEO position in France, leading the Executive Office since October 2023.

My primary goal is to ensure that my executive and her leadership team achieve their strategic objectives. Many people are intrigued by the Chief of Staff role because of its strategic nature and proximity to leadership. But the reality is that success in this role depends on prioritizing effectively and handling the small, often mundane tasks that can bog down your day. Technology has been a lifesaver for me in automating repetitive tasks and freeing up time for what truly matters.

I've also learned to embrace the "good enough" approach. I've stopped striving to be Wonder Woman and started being kinder to myself. After all, I'm only human, and there are only 24 hours in a day. Strategy motivates me, and I make sure to carve out time for it while providing clarity and focus to my team.

■ ■ ■

It sounds like NaY has learned to laugh at perfectionism! We'll explore this further in Chapter 7. The operations function might not have the same shine as the beautifully designed living space of a porch, but make no mistake—it's the backbone of the entire house. These are the problem-solvers, the steady hands that keep everything running. They fix what's broken, maintain the system's integrity, and ensure that the whole thing doesn't just look good but actually works. Garima Gaurav, Senior Program Manager, gives us an inside look at the kind of She it takes to lead critical operations at Microsoft with purpose and a little magic.

The Believer, The Magician

I was born in a small town in Jharkhand, India—a place where life was simple, predictable, and deeply rooted in tradition. The society I grew up in was content with its way of life, and the idea of women working outside the home was rare. It wasn't because women were restricted or denied opportunities, but because life's essentials were comfortably provided. In my family, the prevailing belief was that when you could live a peaceful and comfortable life, there was no need to take orders or instructions from anyone.

But my mother was different. Even now, as I reflect on my journey, I'm reminded of the profound role she has played in shaping who I am. My story would be incomplete without hers. Married at just 18, she had my brother at 19 and me by 20. Being raised in a community that upheld enduring gender role traditions, my mother defied expectations and became my greatest ally—she believed in my potential beyond the limits of convention. She never sought to control my choices but instead stood beside me as a guide and a friend, allowing me to take charge of my own path. Her unwavering faith in me gave me the courage to pursue my passions and reach new heights. Driven by her deep belief in her children, she made it her mission to provide us with the best opportunities and everything we dreamed of. I often called her the "magician" because she didn't just believe in us—she made things happen.

When I think about it now, I realize that through my journey, my mom was quietly living her dreams. She was cheering me on, encouraging me to do the things she couldn't. I was the first woman in my family to step beyond the boundaries of my state—and eventually my country—to follow my dreams. In a society where timelines dictated milestones—when to study, marry, or start a family—I was never questioned about "when." In fact, I once had to ask my family if they ever planned on getting me married!

Over time, I've come to firmly believe that when someone places their utmost trust in you, it creates an invisible sense of responsibility to do the right thing.

Following this principle, I graduated and landed my first job. Seventeen years have passed since I stepped into the corporate world, and what a journey it has been. Some days, it feels like it all happened in a flash; other days, it feels like a lifetime. I started fresh out of school as a developer, eager to learn. Over the years, I transitioned through various roles—database administrator, team leader, service engineer, release manager—and today, I am a program manager who takes pride in building meaningful solutions. Each role has shaped my career, teaching me lessons, delivering triumphs, and confronting me with doubts.

Purpose is a powerful thing. It provides direction when everything else feels uncertain and strength when the journey gets tough. For me, my purpose was fueled by the belief my mom placed in me. It didn't just help me chase my passion; it allowed me to pursue it with fearless determination. I am endlessly grateful for the opportunities I've had—the chance to learn, grow, and evolve both professionally and personally. These experiences, whether successes or challenges, have shaped the person I am today.

Culturally, as women, we are often conditioned to say "yes" and agree to most things. Looking back, I was no different 10 years ago. But my biggest lesson over the years has been the importance of bringing my authentic self to every space—whether personal or professional—and valuing my unique gifts. I've learned to trust my instincts, believe in my abilities, and embrace every part of who I am. Authenticity has allowed me to celebrate my achievements more meaningfully and accept my failures with grace.

These past 17 years have been an incredible chapter. From moving to a new country alone with minimal support to building a life and family here, I've come a long way—but I know the best is yet to come. Of course, there were moments when I felt lost, when doubts crept in, and I questioned everything. But on those tough days, my purpose kept me going.

Once known as the "kid of the project" due to my young age, I often hesitated to speak up, assuming others already knew what I wanted to say. Over time, I've grown into someone who confidently shares her thoughts, embracing my voice with certainty and self-assurance. That growth hasn't always been easy. However, embracing that mindset—being honest about my weaknesses—has been transformative. It has allowed me to identify areas for growth, ask questions, and learn fearlessly.

■ ■ ■

Operations is powered by a purpose-driven She who knows that her work isn't just important—it's essential. She brings her energy, expertise, and grit to keep everything running. And speaking of essentials, let's take a moment to step into the maintenance closet. It's easy to overlook, but it holds the heart of facilities management—the team that makes sure the house doesn't just stand but thrives. They're the ones fixing what's broken, planning the upgrades, and keeping the whole system in motion. Because without them, even the most beautiful spaces wouldn't function.

Step outside, and you'll find the garden—a vibrant, living space that represents partnerships. Just like a real garden, these relationships need care, intention, and collaboration to truly flourish. Here, connections are nurtured, and opportunities grow, benefiting both the organization and its external allies. I find it beautifully symbolic that as we walk through the rooms of the Microsoft house, many women have navigated different spaces in their own careers. I, myself, have had the privilege of moving through operations, engineering, human resources, and now sales—each room shaping me in its own way, teaching me something new about who I am and how I lead. The same is true for Maria Maali. She started in the guest room, a space where she refined her skills, built strong foundations, and prepared for what came next. And when the time was right, she stepped out into the garden. Today, as a Senior Business Development Manager in Microsoft Africa, she doesn't just work in partnerships—she cultivates them.

Blooming Season

One of the most rewarding aspects of my job is witnessing the growth and success of our partners. For example, when I first started my role, I worked with a partner who didn't even have an office space—we used to meet by a swimming pool in the cafeteria. Today, that same partner employs more than 60 people and occupies an entire floor of office space. Their growth not only benefits them but also contributes to Microsoft's success and positively impacts the local economy by creating jobs and driving innovation.

I work closely with our top strategic partners to help them unlock their potential. In many ways, I see myself as a business consultant for our partners, helping them optimize their operations, improve their go-to-market strategies, and achieve greater success. We collaborate to increase their capacity—enhancing their knowledge, hiring the right talent, refining how they communicate their value to customers, and effectively scaling their business.

Fostering partnerships is like building a scaling engine for Microsoft. By empowering our partners, we enable them to deliver even greater value to our customers. I view our partners as an extended team of Microsoft, and their success is deeply tied to ours. Together, we center everything we do around the customer, ensuring that both Microsoft and our partners thrive while delivering exceptional results.

■ ■ ■

Well said, Maria! It's also important to know that for the Microsoft She, it all starts with one essential partnership: the one she builds with herself. When she learns to trust her own voice, own her story, and lead with authenticity, she creates the foundation for every other partnership in her life—inside and outside the organization.

There are so many incredible rooms in this house that I'd love to explore with you in depth, but in the interest of time, let me take you on a quick walk-through—because every space holds its own story, purpose, and power.

The library is where our learning and development teams shine. This is the heart of growth—where employees sharpen skills, spark innovation, and push themselves toward transformation.

Then there's the garage—yes, it's literally called *The Garage*! This is where creativity meets action, where big ideas turn into prototypes, and where passion projects find momentum. The Microsoft Garage is more than a physical space; it's a global program that empowers employees to experiment, collaborate, and bring their ideas to life. Check out Chapter 9 to learn more!

The playroom is all about imagination and collaboration. Here, research and development, brainstorming, and team-building thrive. It's a reminder that play isn't just for kids—it's for anyone looking to unlock creativity, tackle challenges, and rethink possibilities.

The roof represents leadership and governance—the place where vision and strategy come to life. It's where oversight provides guidance, protecting the structure while ensuring alignment and growth. And then there are the attic and basement—the keepers of the past, shaping the future. These spaces hold legacy systems and institutional knowledge—the history that provides stability and continuity. They may not always be the most visible or glamorous, but they're essential.

Just like technology, this house is constantly evolving. New rooms are built, new opportunities emerge, and our understanding of what's possible continues to expand. More than ever, IT isn't just about technical expertise—it's about balancing innovation with human connection. Because at the end of the day, no matter how advanced our tools become, what truly holds the house together is the people inside it.

This chapter is dedicated to showcasing the journeys of both technical and non-technical women in tech. It's a reminder that there's an abundance of rooms—and roles—where your skills are not only transferable but invaluable. And even if you don't have prior experience, there's space for you here, as long as you're ready to bring your unique talents, make an impact, and turn this house into your home. Your dream home.

Chapter Recap

- Your dream house is a space you can transform into a home, both in reality and metaphorically, and you are never limited to just one room!

- Non-technical women have a significant place in tech, bringing transferable skills and making meaningful contributions across diverse roles and functions.

- As technology evolves, the emphasis increasingly lies in blending technical expertise with human connection, empowering individuals to create impact and foster growth in any role they choose.

Embracing the Journey

Think about a spot in your home that could use a little *Feng Shui*—a cluttered closet overflowing with unnecessary items, or that messy drawer where all the miscellaneous odds and ends end up. Take a moment to reclaim that space, rethink its purpose, and transform it into something more intentional and useful. By harmonizing your environment, you can boost energy flow, foster better communication, and create a calming atmosphere that supports your personal growth.

Chapter 4

Diversity: Damned If You Do, Damned If You Don't

Inclusion is not only about who is at the table, but also about ensuring every voice is heard and valued.

—Kathleen Hogan,
Chief People Officer of Microsoft

There's a reason why the Microsoft house allegory from the previous chapter didn't include a dining room. That wasn't an oversight—it was intentional.

For years, the conversation around diversity and inclusion has centered around *the table*: being invited to it, pulling up a chair, or even bringing your own if necessary. The table has long symbolized inclusion—a place where decisions are made, perspectives are shared, and lasting impact is shaped. But when it comes to driving real, systemic change in diversity, equity, and inclusion (DEI), we often find ourselves caught in a paradox: damned if we push forward, damned if we hold back.

The title of this chapter reflects this reality. While experts widely agree that DEI is essential for driving innovation,[1] improving decision-making, increasing productivity, building competitive advantage,[2] fostering brand loyalty, and enhancing economic performance, many corporations continue to struggle with investing in and implementing effective practices. Alarmingly, some have even retreated from

DEI initiatives altogether—a move that could cost businesses billions of dollars[3] and that deprives women every day not only of career opportunities but life opportunities as a whole.

Sarka Kohoutova, Senior Business Program Manager, explains how deeply personal this cost can get.

Without Inclusion, There Is Isolation

"You can have it all," they say. In 2025, education and family are expected—especially for women, where children are part of the equation. I live in the Czech Republic, a place known for free education and long parental leaves. With one child, you can take up to three years and six months off. But is it really a dream? The average parental leave allowance is 9,400 CZK, while rent for a three-bedroom apartment in Prague is around 38,555 CZK. Diapers and formula cost 4,000 CZK. Can you see the disparity? Although our universities are free, only 12% of ICT students in the Czechia are women, and only about 8% of them will work in this field. While long parental leave is an option, it can feel like a trap, not a choice. With limited preschool options for children under 3.5, the cost can be as high as an average salary.

Imagine being a single mother with a flat loan and car payments—that was me 10 years ago, feeling isolated without family support or anyone to relate to.

This issue is close to my heart. I've faced many biases—from family members who didn't believe in a tech career for a girl, to a teacher who discouraged me from attending seminars because I was the only girl there. Even at university, a professor gave me a lower grade than my male peers because, "the world isn't fair, lady." It wasn't until I worked part-time at Microsoft in 2007 that I found my support system and my happy place. After all my experiences, I felt it was time to give back.

I began running Women Mentoring Circles, first for my organization, then for all roles in Czechia and beyond. This initiative has grown rapidly, now covering 25 countries with 220 mentees and 32 captains, with numbers increasing every six months. The circles are diverse beyond gender, bringing together women from various countries, roles, and backgrounds. Beyond mentoring, the biggest benefit is creating a trusted community where you can find advisors, sponsors, allies, and friends.

We've collaborated with external programs focused on women in tech, offering learning sessions, workshops, and networking opportunities. We also provide Microsoft mentors to guide women already in tech or looking to join.

In the end, diversity and inclusion are not just about ticking boxes; they are about creating a world where everyone has the opportunity to thrive. And that is a vision worth fighting for.

■ ■ ■

A Global View of DEI Progress

Across the world, DEI remains a complex challenge:

- In the United States, 48 companies have cut or ended their DEI programs since 2023, including major names like Meta (Facebook), McDonald's, and Nissan, which have significantly scaled back or dismantled their DEI departments.[4]
- Across Europe, progress in DEI remains slow. According to the EY European DEI Index, only 7% of organizations are actively building a genuinely inclusive culture, with an average DEI Index score of just 5.69 out of 10.[5]
- In the Asia-Pacific region, DEI efforts are often highly localized, reflecting the specific needs of different countries and communities.[6] While there are successes, significant challenges persist in achieving gender parity and advancing LGBTQ+ rights.[7]

- In Africa, DEI initiatives often involve collaborations between businesses and governments. The continent's vast cultural diversity presents unique opportunities and challenges, as inclusivity efforts must respect the varied identities of its communities.[8]
- In Latin America, DEI efforts are shaped by the region's history of colonialism and slavery, with deeply entrenched racial hierarchies and income inequality posing significant challenges. The region's cultural diversity requires tailored strategies that celebrate its rich array of languages and traditions. However, competing interests among marginalized groups, such as indigenous and Afro-Latino communities, can complicate these efforts.[9]

The reality is clear: while the journey toward real progress in DEI is complex, the benefits are undeniable. The real challenge isn't in recognizing the need for change—it's in translating good intentions into lasting action. At Microsoft, like in so many organizations, the company's DEI efforts have evolved over time. And while there is always more work to do, I'm proud to know that the momentum continues to move in the right direction—even in the face of the sobering statistics I just shared. Microsoft's 2024 Global Diversity & Inclusion Report[10] tells us that we are making meaningful progress. But when I ask myself why, the answer goes beyond leadership initiatives or corporate investments. The true driving force behind this progress is people.

In the early days, Microsoft—like so many companies of its time—was singularly focused on growth. As the company expanded, so did the diversity of its employees. Leadership increasingly prioritized DEI, but the real shift happened because people refused to be passive observers. They saw gaps and created solutions. They built Employee Resource Groups (ERGs), raised their voices, and challenged outdated norms. Step by step, they helped break down entrenched barriers and redefined what inclusive leadership looks like.

Aja Hill, Director of Cloud Solution Architects and Women Chapter WW Co-Chair, is one of those changemakers.

Owning My Space in DEI Leadership

I've been at Microsoft since 2008, and during this time, I've come to understand that diversity and inclusion aren't just moral imperatives—they are essential to our success. As a global company serving a diverse customer base, we need varied perspectives shaping our products and strategies to truly meet their needs.

Reflecting on my journey, one of the most pivotal decisions I made was joining and eventually leading WAM, the Women at Microsoft Employee Resource Group. Initially, I hesitated. As a Black woman, I wasn't sure if WAM was the right space for me. My deep connection to BAM, Blacks at Microsoft, had always felt like home, and I believed my efforts should remain focused there. I also worried about how it might appear—would prioritizing women's issues seem like I was leaving the Black community behind?

After thoughtful reflection, I realized I didn't have to choose one over the other. My identity as a Black woman gave me the unique opportunity to contribute meaningfully to both communities. Embracing leadership in WAM didn't diminish my commitment to BAM; instead, it allowed me to bring my full self to both spaces. I've worked intentionally to ensure that my leadership in WAM encourages others, especially women of color, to see themselves as part of this community as well.

Microsoft has offered a unique environment in terms of diversity. Coming from spaces that were either predominantly White or Black, it's been refreshing to work in a place where people from so many different backgrounds interact. That said, there's still room to grow. While I've seen genuine commitment to diversity, systemic change requires time, accountability, and continuous effort at every level of leadership.

Some moments in my career have been profoundly rewarding. One such highlight was participating in the NASDAQ bell-ringing ceremony. Standing there, I reflected on how far women have come. Just a few decades ago, women couldn't even open a bank account in their own name—and now, here we were, standing at one of the world's most iconic financial institutions, representing progress and potential.

Another proud moment was inviting America Ferrera—a celebrated actress and advocate for women's rights, gender equality, immigration reform, racial justice, and environmental conservation—to one of our initiatives. Her powerful speech captured the shared experiences and challenges of so many women. It was deeply fulfilling to amplify her voice, knowing how impactful her words would be.

But of course, challenges remain. I've noticed a decline in some of our external initiatives aimed at inspiring the next generation, like the DigiGirlz program we once had. While our Women at Microsoft Scholarships are a great start, I believe we can do more. Imagine offering mentorships, internships, or even direct career opportunities for scholarship recipients—truly investing in their futures rather than making one-time gestures.

Looking ahead, I think about the next generation and the importance of representation. My ultimate career goal is to serve as a Fortune 100 board member, and that ambition is rooted in my desire to inspire young Black girls. I want them to see someone who looks like them achieving remarkable things and know it's possible for them, too.

Whether through BAM, WAM, or other initiatives, I'm committed to creating spaces where everyone can show up authentically and without fear. At the end of the day, I'm driven by the hope that the work I do today will inspire and uplift others tomorrow.

Representation matters, and I believe deeply in its power to transform lives and shape a better world.

■ ■ ■

Aja's story reminds us that a table is just a piece of wood until people make the intention to gather together around it. As Miri often says, "Inclusion starts with *I*." It's people who shape culture, and culture is what ultimately drives DEI. But this relationship between individuals and community isn't always simple. Each of us brings our own experiences, talents, and expectations to the table, making the work of building an inclusive culture both meaningful and complex. Ginniee Sahi, former Global Accounts Leader, confirms this important truth.

Meet Me at the Tree House

My journey as a woman of color in tech has been a blend of humor, resilience, and growth—a story of breaking barriers and redefining spaces that weren't always built for someone like me. From the "cowboy culture" at Oracle Global to the business-focused environment at Salesforce, and then leading global accounts at Microsoft, I've seen firsthand how inclusion—or the lack of it—can shape lives and careers.

I still vividly remember my interview at Microsoft with the hiring manager, who was based in Germany. Our conversations were a mix of Teams chats, Skype messages, and emails, layered with professionalism and humor. From the beginning, he set the tone by asking how I wanted to be treated and ensuring I felt valued and respected. That respect laid the foundation for a career where I've been able to win customers, drive impact, and grow as a leader.

As a brown woman, standing just 5'3", I've faced my share of challenges. But I've learned that those differences—the ones that sometimes make you feel like an outsider—can also be your superpower. Whether it was navigating Executive Briefing Centers, touring data centers, or collaborating with teams from around the world, I saw how my perspective added value.

At Microsoft, creativity thrives in unexpected spaces. I often found myself working with customers in the tree houses (yes, we have tree houses!), far removed from traditional boardrooms. There, surrounded by nature, I realized that inclusion isn't just a concept—it's a practice. It's about a daily, individual intention to create spaces where everyone, regardless of who they are or where they come from, can contribute and feel empowered.

In every role I've held, I've leaned into the power of listening—really listening. Understanding different perspectives has allowed me to connect with customers, partners, and teams on a deeper level. Every interaction, from presenting at EBCs (Executive Briefing Centers) to brainstorming over coffee, has been an opportunity to amplify voices and co-create solutions that matter.

Empowerment isn't just a word; it's a way of being. Whether leading hackathons, engaging with C-level executives, or mentoring young talent, I've seen how meaningful action can create ripples of change. Technology has the power to transform lives, but it's the people behind it who make that transformation real.

Even the small moments—like having coffee meetings with Microsoft's colorful logo on the cups—remind me of the magic that happens when collaboration and creativity intersect. It's in those seemingly ordinary spaces that extraordinary ideas often take root.

As I consider my growth, I realize how much my story has been shaped by the people who believed in me and the opportunities that inclusion made possible. But let's be honest: being a woman of color in a space dominated by others isn't always easy. There are moments when we feel invisible, when our voice gets lost in the crowd. But those moments are also a call to action—to keep showing up, to keep advocating for representation. And if the right space doesn't exist, create one. Build a place where diversity and creativity are not just welcomed, but celebrated. Preferably, a tree house!

■ ■ ■

Creating space and inviting people to the table may seem like an obvious step, yet the challenge remains. Perhaps the issue isn't just the table itself, but the personal and collective wounds that keep individuals from fully showing up and participating.

Through conversations with colleagues across the tech industry, it's clear that the struggle with DEI isn't just an institutional one—it's also deeply personal. If culture is shaped by people—the ones who stand beside leadership, drive initiatives, and advocate for themselves—then it's not entirely fair to place the burden solely on organizations. There's an opportunity here to look inward, to examine the historical and present-day barriers that hold us back. But even more importantly, there's an opportunity to transform that pain into purpose.

Turning wounds into action isn't just possible—it's powerful. Just look at Lisanne Brons, Global Black Belt M365 Copilot, who channeled her frustration with inequality into a mission to uplift others, helping them feel confident, included, and valued.

Tell Me I Can't, Then Watch Me

At Microsoft, we define thriving as to be energized and empowered to do meaningful work. When people thrive, this leads to better business outcomes. And therefore it's really simple: investing in an inclusive culture will help people and businesses become more successful.

Since I was little, I've embraced the playful and fearless mindset of Pippi Longstocking, the beloved fictional character created by Swedish author Astrid Lindgren: "I've never done it, but I think I can." People often described me as a curious, adventurous girl who loved to learn. But as I grew older, my inner Pippi grew a bit frustrated. Despite having a loving family and a great childhood, I began noticing subtle yet pervasive messages that women were seen as less than men in the workplace. It was in the way my dad spoke about his job versus my mom's, the "dumb blond" jokes that were common in the Netherlands, or how math and science were often portrayed as "for boys." Even TV shows seemed to cast women as second-class citizens at work.

This realization sparked a stubbornness in me: *Why would you assume I can't do it?* That stubbornness turned into anger, which became a driving force during my younger years. I was determined to prove the world wrong.

What followed was an adventurous decade: I studied AI, traveled the world, and joined Microsoft. The determination to show people I could play at the "champions league" level never left me. When I chose to study AI, I heard comments like, "Are you sure?" or "Isn't that a boy's field?" At the time, those words had a significant impact, fueling my determination to excel. I worked hard to prove them wrong, and as my confidence grew, I began to see those doubts as opportunities.

At Microsoft, I shifted my mindset. Instead of feeling insecure when customers underestimated me because I was a young woman, I started to enjoy the underdog position. Go ahead, underestimate me . . . I'll show you what I've got.

When the anger subsided, what remained was a strong belief: everyone is unique, and pretending to be something you're not won't get you anywhere. I learned to embrace being the different one—the youngest, the only woman, the least technical. Owning my uniqueness helped me understand that everyone brings their own skills, experiences, and perspectives to the table, and that's what leads to amazing outcomes.

This belief shaped how I approached my career. I took on roles in tech, sales, business strategy, and leadership with a simple mindset: I'll figure out how to make this role my own. I studied what others did, read the role descriptions, completed the necessary training, but ultimately defined success in terms of my unique impact.

Over time, my focus shifted from proving others wrong to taking control of my career and leading with my strengths. I created a personal mission statement: To lead people into a world of new opportunities, help them achieve things they've never done before, and build success together.

This mission has guided every role I've taken. As a technical specialist, I introduced customers to the cloud. As a manager, I coached people to reach their full potential. As a scuba diving instructor, I opened others to the underwater world. Now, as a mother, I get to join my daughter in her exploration of life.

Living by this mission has given my career purpose and meaning. It also reinforced my belief that people are most powerful when they lead from the heart rather than just following a job description.

As I grew into leadership roles, I became more curious about company culture. How do you create an environment where people feel valued? How do you ensure everyone can show up as their best selves? Thanks to Rawan Shalhoub, the HR director of Microsoft Netherlands at the time, I had the chance to help set up local Employee Resource Groups (ERGs). Leading the Gender Equality ERG and participating in women-in-tech initiatives allowed me to coach young women, advocate for inclusion, and even serve as a confidential counselor for colleagues navigating workplace challenges.

Through these experiences, I've learned some valuable lessons:

> **Curiosity fuels inclusion:** The way you experience the world is different from how others do. There isn't one universal truth; staying curious helps bridge gaps and uncover others' lived experiences.

- **Assume good intentions:** While not always foolproof, this mindset helps maintain positivity. Jumping to conclusions about others' words or actions rarely leads to progress.
- **Don't be naive:** Issues like harassment and discrimination are real, even within organizations like Microsoft. Stay aware, call out problems when necessary, and work toward creating safe spaces for everyone.
- **Challenge your assumptions:** Recognize your own privileges and biases to ensure they don't limit your perspective.
- **Make DEI engaging:** I've always avoided being the "DEI police." Instead, I focus on fun, meaningful activities that raise awareness and foster connection.
- **Action is essential:** Diversity, equity, and inclusion require effort. Believing in the cause isn't enough—you need to actively do the work.
- **Repetition matters:** DEI isn't a one-time effort. It's a continuous journey that requires consistent focus to avoid backsliding.
- **Managers make the difference:** The biggest influence on someone's workplace experience is their direct manager. Leadership sets the tone for culture.

■ ■ ■

Real, lasting change in diversity, equity, and inclusion takes both institutions and individuals. At a personal level, the She has been learning to turn her pain into purpose and work to heal her wounds—but that alone isn't enough. She must also channel those deep emotions into fuel for action, using her experiences as motivation to drive change. There's still so much more to do. That means stepping into leadership, finding opportunities to challenge the status quo, and using her voices to push for the progress we all deserve. Pooja Sund, Principal PM Manager, is a prime example.

Be Bold, Be Brave, Be You!

As a woman in tech leadership, I bring a unique blend of perspectives that fuel creativity and inclusivity in problem-solving. I'm honored to be recognized as a LinkedIn Top Voice and Women in Tech Contributor, a Hall of Fame inductee for Global Women in Tech 2023, and a finance and engineering leader at Microsoft. But above all, I see myself as a champion for diversity and inclusion (D&I), committed to creating environments where everyone has the opportunity to thrive.

While my professional achievements reflect my expertise and leadership, the work I'm most passionate about happens within Microsoft's Employee Resource Groups (ERGs). Over the years, I've had the privilege of holding leadership roles in WAM, C&E and Commerce & Finance Services (CFS) women communities. These roles have allowed me to help shape a culture of inclusion, authenticity, and opportunity for women at Microsoft. For me, these efforts are deeply personal. Even after 19 years at Microsoft (15 as a full-time employee and 4 as a vendor), I know my journey to help build an inclusive, empowering workplace is far from over. I've formed deep, trusted bonds with fellow ERG leaders, where we celebrate victories, share challenges, and support one another through it all. Beyond professional development, our ERGs foster a true sense of belonging through community events, storytelling sessions, and informal networking opportunities. But this work extends beyond Microsoft—it's for the entire tech industry. Every organization, every team, every leader has the power to drive change. It starts with a single conversation, a single initiative, a single opportunity to connect and uplift. From there, it grows into something much larger. For me, this journey is more than a career—it's a calling. It's about creating spaces where women feel valued, heard, and empowered to lead. It's about leaving a legacy of inclusion that will inspire generations to come. And through it all, I stand by my personal mantra: Be Bold, Be Brave, and Be You.

■ ■ ■

Reflecting on these stories—each centered around the idea of the table as a gathering place where we all belong—I was reminded of a writing exercise a friend shared from a retreat. The prompt was simple yet profound: Choose a piece of furniture in your home, describe it in detail, and through that description, reveal where you are in time—your age, your stage of life. She had just five minutes to write, and here's what she captured:

My Timber Sister Wife

Sturdy and elegant stands the old, rugged dining table. Heavy. Shiny. The wear and tear suit her well. By any means, this isn't her first home, but it will be her last. She has surely graced other abodes with her statuesque and traditional presence. She stands tall and commands attention in her raw, cedar wood. The cracks in between the thick timber hold invisible prayers, wishes, conversations. Her long, beautiful legs made of bamboo and carved in floral detail with woodwork mastery and design adorn the "highlights and lowlights" of the clan. The boys jump happily and almost ceremoniously around it with big boy energy, admiring its statuesque presence and probably already machinating ways to make it serve as a fort. My husband stares at it with pride. A woodworker himself, he understands the deep value of carpentry art. I stare at her knowing she is an accomplice to me. She will help nurture our home when I fall short as a wife and mother. She will keep the boys company as I cook in the kitchen and they do their homework. She will ground the fights over bills between my husband and I when we do our budget. She will serve as refuge for Max, our new puppy. She will be more than a dining table. She will be the gathering place for all things life and memories at our home.

■ ■ ■

It's no surprise that, out of the 15 writers at that retreat, 8 chose their dining tables as the focal point of their stories. The dining table isn't just furniture, nor is it merely a metaphor for inclusion. It's a sacred space—a place where we all long to serve and be served, to see and be seen, to love and be loved. And yet, when it comes to breaking down the barriers that deny some of us a seat at the table, it feels like we're damned if we do and damned if we don't.

Damned if we push to move longstanding boundaries, if we let our righteous anger fuel our fight against the pervasive inequalities that linger. Damned if we speak up, speak out, or even dare to find our voice in spaces that were not designed for us. Because the world isn't fully ready for it, and the journey toward harmony and justice is long and grueling.

Some of us carry wounds too deep to articulate. Some of us are scared, silenced by a lifetime of being told we don't belong. Some of us have been victims of the harsh, undeniable reality that inequality is not a thing of the past—it is alive and thriving in systems, in cultures, in policies, and even in homes.

But damned if we don't. Because if we don't, we fail those who come after us. We make it harder—not easier—for the next generation to rise, to claim their place, to feel like they belong. If we allow exhaustion, fear, or pain to hold us back, if we refuse to channel our struggles into meaningful action, we surrender the fight for justice and equality.

The dining table, in all its symbolism, reminds us that change begins with gathering, with coming together. It is in these moments—sharing space, stories, and struggles—that we find the courage to keep going.

It is where we remember that, though the journey is long, we are not walking it alone.

So, damned if we do and damned if we don't. But we must. We must push, we must speak, and stand our ground—not just for ourselves, but for the generations that will sit at this table after us.

> **Chapter Recap**
>
> - Diversity, equity, and inclusion isn't just about having a seat at the table; it's about making room for others, breaking down barriers, and fostering the kind of meaningful dialogue that leads to real progress.
>
> - Advancing DEI is not easy work. It requires deliberate effort, especially in the face of deep-seated systemic challenges. And yet, the greatest risk of all is inaction.
>
> - Real progress begins with both personal and collective accountability. It happens when we transform pain into purpose, when we use our voices to advocate for change, and when we recognize that the responsibility doesn't rest solely on institutions, but on all of us.

> **Inspiration for the Journey**
>
> Do you have a table where you're creating space for other women? Whether you're giving a talk, leading a project, or working on something that could involve a broader team, being intentional about inviting women to participate matters. It's how we foster visibility, strengthen collaboration, and build a collective effort to uplift and support one another.

Chapter 5
Resilience and the Bias Monster

I hope you will go out and let stories, that is life, happen to you, and that you will work with these stories . . . water them with your blood and tears and your laughter till they bloom, till you yourself burst into bloom.
—Clarissa Pinkola Estés

I was in Italy, minding my own business, savoring a scrumptious bowl of pasta, when I noticed a shiny new book sitting on the coffee table of my Airbnb. Being both a writer and a voracious reader—and knowing my husband is neither—I assumed the book was meant for me. Naturally, I grabbed it, took it outside, and continued eating my pasta while flipping through its pages.

Rarely does a book catch me off guard. As a writer, I'm usually guilty of overanalyzing everything I read—predicting the author's next move, dissecting their choices, and, honestly, sometimes spoiling the magic for myself. I even have the audacity to read magazines backward (I know, it's odd), and I'm not above skipping chapters in books if I think the next one might be juicier. I always circle back, of course, but only on my terms.

So, imagine my surprise when this book, *Women Who Run with the Wolves* by Clarissa Pinkola Estés, completely disarmed me. It didn't offer a gentle invitation to reflect; it yanked me right out of my usual patterns and sent me sprinting. And here's the kicker: it wasn't even my book. Didn't buy it, didn't seek it out. But somehow, in that deep, soul-knowing way, it was always meant for me.

This book didn't just challenge me—it nourished me. It called me to the kind of deep reflection that's both uncomfortable and transformative. At its core, it reshaped my understanding of resilience. Because resilience isn't just about enduring the hard stuff—it's about embracing the stories life hands us, letting them settle into our bones, and allowing them to shape us in ways we never saw coming. It's about growing, not despite the struggles, but *because* of them.

Throughout history, women have pushed forward, marking milestones that redefined what's possible—Oberlin College admitting women in 1833, the Equal Pay Act of 1963, Swiss women securing the right to vote in 1971, and Saudi Arabia lifting the ban on women driving in 2018. Each victory has been hard-won, a testament to perseverance and courage. But let's be clear—the journey is far from over.

From the time we are little girls, we are taught to be kind. To be agreeable. To put others first. And while these lessons often come wrapped in love and good intentions, they can also come at a cost. They shape how we move through the world, teaching us to make ourselves smaller, to avoid conflict, to keep the peace—even when the peace comes at the expense of our own needs, our own voice, our own worth.

We learn to say "I'm sorry" before we even know what we're apologizing for. We hesitate to take up space, to say no, to stand in our power. And over time, these patterns become more than just behaviors—they become beliefs. We start to believe that our value is tied to how likable we are. That our success depends on how well we fit in. That our strength is something to be softened, rather than something to be celebrated.

But here's the truth: real strength isn't about making ourselves more palatable—it's about embracing who we are, fully and unapologetically. Eleanor Roosevelt once said, "A woman is like a teabag—you can't tell how strong she is until you put her in hot water." And she was right. Women have always been strong. We have always been resilient. Like wolves in the wild, we have learned to adapt, to endure, to turn struggle into strength. But resilience isn't just about survival. It's about rising. It's about standing tall in the spaces where we've been told to shrink.

Women have always been a symbol of resilience—instinctive, adaptive, and undeniably courageous. Like the wild wolves in *Women Who Run with the Wolves*, we carry a strength that is both innate and hard-earned, rooted in intuition, perseverance, and a deep connection to our untamed, authentic selves. We've pushed back against expectations, broken through barriers, and carved out spaces where none existed before. Time and again, we've proven that resilience isn't just about survival—it's about rising, reclaiming, and thriving.

The challenge is in the workplace, in leadership, in industries where we are still the exception rather than the rule, that wildness—the very thing that makes us powerful—can feel like something we have to tame. We second guess ourselves. We hesitate to push back.

Whether it's the kind we are born with or the kind we build over time, resilience is what allows us to stand firm in a world that sometimes tells us to sit down. It's what gives us the courage to raise our hands, take the risks, and carve our own paths. It's what turns pain into purpose, struggle into strength. And perhaps most importantly, resilience is what reminds us that our stories—the messy, complicated, beautiful stories of who we are—deserve to be told, despite the Bias Monster that plagues us.

Natalia Nikonenko, Senior Technical Specialist, shares her personal encounter with this monster.

The Deadliest Bias: Self-Doubt

Biases come in many forms—shaping our views, perceptions, and decisions. Often, when we think of bias, we discuss it in the context of how we view others: their culture, race, gender, education, or beliefs. Rarely, however, do we turn the lens inward to examine the biases we hold about ourselves. Yet, these internal biases can be the most damaging, quietly influencing our self-worth and decisions in profound ways. This is exactly where my story begins.

My corporate career has been deeply intertwined with my personal journey. Before joining Microsoft, I ended a long-term relationship that, in hindsight, was both toxic and mentally abusive. My partner was not just my colleague but someone I managed, adding layers of complexity to an already challenging situation. Over the years, I was repeatedly told by my partner that I wasn't knowledgeable, that I was a poor manager, and, ultimately, that I was only hired because of my partner's influence. Repeatedly hearing these words from someone I trusted, I began to believe them. My self-esteem plummeted, and I became dependent on someone who undermined me at every turn. It was a disaster, but one day, I decided it was enough. I found the strength to end the relationship, though the process was excruciating.

Despite moving countries to escape the situation, my internalized biases lingered. I had convinced myself I was unworthy and incapable of anything new. My new partner saw my struggles and encouraged me to seek a different path, but I resisted, repeating the lies I had internalized: "I know nothing," "I can't do this," "No one will hire me." But with persistent encouragement, I pursued professional training, earned new certifications, and eventually took a leap of faith—I quit my job.

As I searched for new opportunities, I applied to Microsoft, more as a "what if" than a real expectation. To my surprise, I was invited to interview. One round turned into another, and then three more. Each time, I received positive feedback. I was stunned. Could I really be worth hiring? It was a perspective I hadn't considered for myself in years. To my amazement, I received an offer—but there was a twist: I discovered I was pregnant.

I wrestled with my emotions, convinced that my personal news would derail the hiring process. Who would hire a pregnant woman? But honesty and transparency on such an important topic felt like the only path, so I called the recruiter. What happened next shattered my assumptions: my recruiter and hiring manager reassured me that my pregnancy wouldn't affect their decision. "You're worth it," they told me. Those words echoed in my mind, challenging everything I thought I knew about myself and the workplace.

I joined Microsoft, welcomed by an incredible team of professionals. I worked until my maternity leave, and after my son was born, I returned early—not because I had to, but because I wanted to. The experience blended my personal and professional lives in ways I couldn't have imagined, teaching me a powerful lesson about self-bias and the importance of confronting it.

Over the past five years at Microsoft, I've had multiple managers, taken on various roles, and worked with inspiring people. My work has been recognized and celebrated—not once have I heard that I'm not good enough. Looking back, I realize how close I came to missing these opportunities simply because I believed the false narratives I had internalized. My biases nearly deprived me of a fulfilling career and personal growth.

Self-biases are particularly challenging because they're deeply personal and often invisible to others. Unlike external biases, which can be called out and addressed, self-bias requires us to recognize, confront, and challenge our own assumptions. This is not an easy task, but it is a necessary one.

■ ■ ■

Natalia's story shines a light on a kind of bias we don't often name—the one that lives quietly inside us. When we talk about bias, we tend to picture it as something out there—an external force that holds us back, makes us feel small, slams doors in our faces. But Natalia's journey reminds us of a deeper truth: the Bias Monster isn't always lurking in the world around us. Sometimes, it's whispering from within.

And sometimes, the Bias Monster isn't always the villain.

Take Shira Fayans, former COO and CMO of Microsoft Israel. She was labeled a "Bossy Woman" by some of her colleagues, but instead of shrinking back, she led with courage and grace. Shira recognized that bias isn't always about personal prejudice—it's baked into the systems and institutions we're part of. Yet it is those same limiting systems that can also inspire us to lead differently.

The Bias Monster Isn't Always a Villain

In every organization, transformation isn't just a series of new technologies or processes. It's about people, culture, and the invisible forces that either push you forward or hold you back. When I took on the mantle of driving Microsoft's cloud transformation, I wasn't just grappling with technical roadblocks but facing an even bigger enemy: the entrenched biases of the organization itself. The "Bias Monster," as I came to call it, showed up in countless ways—old habits, outdated thinking, and yes, even the fear of failure. But at Microsoft, we had the will to overcome it, especially because there was an army of resilient women willing to face it head-on.

Resilience is the foundation of transformation—an unwavering belief in what's possible, paired with the ability to adapt when reality demands it. In my years leading Microsoft's cloud transformation, particularly in Israel, I've come to understand that resilience doesn't manifest as an all-out battle against the past or its limitations. Instead, it emerges in the quiet moments of decision-making when you choose to engage with what is, not as a barrier, but as a foundation to build upon.

This story is about those decisions—how we navigated a world that wasn't always ready for change and how we built new paths when none existed. Our journey wasn't driven by the need to tear down the old but by the realization that to move forward, we had to rethink, reframe, and realign. The road to cloud transformation didn't just require technical innovation; it required a cultural shift—an expansion of how we viewed ourselves, our partners, and our customers. It was in those moments of recalibration that resilience took on a new meaning.

The Cloud Transformation: A New Era for Microsoft

When I first took on the responsibility of driving Microsoft's cloud transformation in Israel, it became apparent that we weren't truly ready. Our legacy as a tech giant was unquestionable, but there was an underlying complacency that made transformation harder than it needed to be. It wasn't that we didn't have the technical ability—Microsoft has always been at the forefront of technology—but our internal muscle memory was rooted in the past.

In a world rapidly shifting toward cloud-first thinking, we were still operating with old-world habits. Our processes, relationships, and even how we defined success had become too rigid. The ecosystem around us—startups, venture capitalists, innovators—saw Microsoft as reliable, yes, but not dynamic enough to be part of their next chapter.

To them, we were legacy infrastructure, not cutting-edge enablers of innovation. They didn't see us as the cloud partner of the future.

It was a sobering realization. The challenge we faced wasn't just external; it was deeply internal. We needed to transform the way we operated at a core level. The solution, I realized, could not come from technical advancements alone. It needed to be cultural, philosophical. We needed to build new muscles, not just new technology. The tools we had weren't wrong—they were simply not enough for where we were headed.

One of the first shifts was in how we sold. In Israel, the enterprise culture was deeply entrenched in the EA (Enterprise Agreement) model. Moving to direct sales felt like an uphill battle, and not just for our customers, but for our own teams. The local culture had a bias toward what had always worked—EA agreements were long-term, stable, and familiar. The prospect of a direct sales model, especially in such a small and close-knit market, was unsettling.

But I saw it differently. This wasn't about replacing one model with another; it was about learning. I decided that we needed to approach this with humility. We couldn't afford to dictate the terms from the top down. We needed to become a student of the market, to understand the new customer journey.

When I visited corporate, I met with an incubation team that was experimenting with direct cloud sales. They, too, were facing significant challenges. In that room, I saw an opportunity—not to compete but to collaborate. I offered to pilot the direct sales model in Israel, leveraging the startup ecosystem that had defined so much of our tech evolution. My proposal was simple: let's treat this as a partnership. We would invest in learning together, through trial and error. We would test the waters, iterate, and evolve. No grand plans, just small, meaningful steps forward.

The first year was hard. There were no immediate wins, no headlines celebrating a breakthrough. But that's the thing about resilience—it doesn't need instant gratification. It's about laying the groundwork for sustained growth. By year two, we had hit our stride. Our growth increased 10-fold. By year three, the largest startup on Azure in Israel had begun with the direct sales model. What had once seemed like a risky bet had become a success story, not just for Israel, but for the entire company. This approach became a blueprint for how Microsoft could think globally about cloud sales, and I was honored with a creativity marketing award. But more than the recognition, it was proof that transformation begins when we have the courage to step into the unknown with a willingness to learn.

Building Agility: From Tradition to Transformation

Transformation isn't about discarding the past; it's about evolving beyond it. One of the greatest lessons I learned early on is that you can't win alone. At Microsoft, we've always celebrated individual success, but in moments of true transformation, the power of community far exceeds individual contribution. Transformation is about people—about internal teams, external partners, and ecosystems—and it requires an agile mindset that isn't afraid to build relationships and cross boundaries.

In Israel, the sales force was deeply rooted in traditional methods. With enterprise sales thriving, no one was in a rush to shake things up. It wasn't that they were resistant to change; they simply didn't see the need for it. The system was running well; why disrupt it? But I knew that the growth we were seeing in traditional sales was just the surface. The real opportunity lay in creating new kinds of relationships, in going beyond the transactional nature of enterprise agreements and building lasting partnerships that were focused on innovation and co-creation.

On one of my first visits to Microsoft's headquarters, I set a personal goal: I would meet as many people as I could, not caring about titles or hierarchies, but about shared interests. I was determined to build a coalition, not just of decision-makers but of visionaries—people who could see the future we were trying to create. In one of those meetings, I laid out my vision for Israel's cloud transformation. Within 24 hours, I secured direct investment from corporate—a first for Israel. It wasn't just about the money; it was about commitment. We had the backing to go big, and that made all the difference.

Going big isn't just about resources, though—it's about mindset. When I heard that Israel wasn't included in the Ignite Tour, a global event focused on cloud transformation, I saw an opportunity. Israel may be a small market, but it's one defined by its innovation and its startup culture. I went through the org chart, identified the key stakeholders, and reached out directly. I shared my vision for how Israel could be a crucial stop on the tour, not just because of its size but because of its significance. And it worked. Israel became part of the tour, and the impact was profound—not just for the event but for how Israel's role in the cloud ecosystem was perceived internally and externally. It was a moment of storytelling, of creating a narrative that resonated beyond the numbers.

People-First Obsession: Rethinking Customer Engagement

In all of these transformations, one theme stands out: the importance of people. The technology may change, but it's the relationships—the human connections—that drive real innovation. Cloud adoption isn't just about offering the best product; it's about understanding the journey your customers are on and partnering with them every step of the way.

For Microsoft in Israel, this meant rethinking how we approached startups. Selling to large enterprises was familiar territory. We had the relationships, the contracts, the processes down to a science. But startups were different. They moved faster, operated with greater intensity, and were relentless in their pursuit of innovation. Our traditional selling model wouldn't work here. We needed a different approach, one rooted in empathy and partnership.

I spent countless hours meeting with startups, not to sell them on Microsoft but to listen. I wanted to understand their culture, their needs, their aspirations. What I learned was that they weren't looking for a vendor; they were looking for a partner. Someone who understood that their success was our success. Slowly, we began to build a new kind of relationship with these companies—one based on shared vision rather than a transaction. And as those relationships deepened, we were able to transform the enterprise-focus from a barrier into an advantage. We had what startups needed: scale, stability, and expertise. All we had to do was reframe how we delivered it.

A New Kind of Leadership: Impact Over Ego

At the heart of this chapter is the principle that leadership in transformation isn't about ego or power; it's about creating impact. The women of Microsoft, myself included, have learned that the most profound changes happen not when we fight against the old but when we embrace the new with humility, courage, and a commitment to learning.

Resilience isn't about pushing back at every obstacle; it's about knowing when to pivot, when to adapt, and when to engage others in the journey. The Bias Monster isn't always a villain to be slain—it's often a reminder of the work still left to do. Each challenge we faced in transforming Microsoft's cloud business wasn't an indictment of the past; it was an invitation to build the future.

This is the power of transformation: it doesn't happen in isolation. It happens when we learn together, when we build coalitions, and when we dare to dream beyond what is comfortable and familiar. That's how we create lasting impact. That's how we embrace resilience.

■ ■ ■

Bravissima, Shira! In 2019, Shira received the Microsoft WW Champion Award for founding the Microsoft Blockchain Academy, a program that offered hands-on, practical training. Year after year, she earned the highest management scores from her direct reports—each one of them growing into Key Talents under her leadership. Microsoft Corporate took notice, selecting her as a Champion for the EMEA MACH MBA recruitment team and inviting her to join an exclusive group of managerial coaches. And she didn't stop there. Shira became a global mentor for managers, sharing her wisdom and guiding leaders around the world. If that's not resilience in a bottle, I don't know what is.

To wrap up this chapter, here's one last story on resilience—along with some powerful personal tips—that beautifully captures the raw, untamed power of rising strong. Clarissa Pinkola Estés, in *Women Who Run with the Wolves*, describes resilience as the wildness within us—the deep, instinctual knowing that tells us when to fight, when to heal, and when to push forward despite the odds. It's the wolf inside us that refuses to be tamed, that trusts its own voice, that stands its ground when the world tells it to shrink. Here to take us on the journey of finding that wolf within and rising above is Sonia Wadhwa, Senior Director at Microsoft.

Resilience Is the Ultimate Wolf Skill

If I were to sum up the secret to success in one word, it would be "resilience." This invaluable quality was instilled in me by my mother, who navigated through the biases, criticisms, and hurdles of the 1970s and 1980s with grace and determination. Watching her rise above challenges taught me the importance of picking myself up after every fall, learning from experiences, and emerging stronger with each setback. Her strength and perseverance became the foundation of the values that shaped my career and guide me to this day.

Early Career Challenges

My first job was nothing short of a baptism by fire. Shortly after taking a few weeks off for my wedding, I faced unexpected biases. In a workplace where personal milestones like marriage were seen as distractions, I was labeled "non-serious" about my career. This label denied me opportunities, and my performance reviews suffered as a result.

But I refused to accept this unfairness. I challenged my leader to let me prove my commitment and was given extra-credit projects as a test. Within months, I excelled, demonstrating my skills and determination. When I left that company a year later for a bigger opportunity, my manager admitted, "Sonia, not recognizing your potential and skills was one of the biggest mistakes of my career."

From Cowering to Surviving at Microsoft

Joining Microsoft was a dream come true, but it came with its own challenges. I landed in a toxic team with an angry, biased manager. Nearly every day, I found myself shrinking under the fear of my actions being second-guessed or being reprimanded. One particularly tough day, after being publicly berated in a hallway, I sat in my car feeling completely defeated.

It was then that I thought of my mother—her strength, her resilience—and realized I couldn't let this situation define me. I resolved to focus on my long-term goals, to grow beyond this experience, and to find my way out of this situation with confidence and grace.

Rebuilding Confidence and Finding Community

Each day, I worked to rebuild my confidence. I explored new skills, sought training, and connected with experts to better understand different roles and opportunities. Gradually, I found a community of women who were at similar career stages. Together, we shared stories, provided support, and encouraged one another to keep pushing forward.

These conversations helped me recognize my own strengths, like my ability to bring order to chaos with empathy. This reflection allowed me to pivot my career intentionally, ultimately leading me to roles like Chief of Staff, where I could leverage those strengths.

Thriving and Helping Others Thrive

Over the next eight years, I transitioned from merely surviving to thriving. I advanced in my career, exploring diverse roles that expanded my leadership and business acumen. During this time, my passion for mentorship grew. It became clear that my purpose was to pave the way for others to thrive alongside me.

One of the most fulfilling experiences of my career has been mentoring more than 500 women through a program I developed. This passion also led to the honor of co-chairing Microsoft's largest Employee Resource Group, Women at Microsoft, where I continue to support and uplift others.

Tips for Building Resilience

Resilience is a vital skill in the technology industry, particularly for women navigating biases and challenges. Here are my key takeaways:

- **Cultivate a Growth Mindset:** Treat challenges as opportunities to learn and grow.
- **Build a Support Network:** Surround yourself with mentors, allies, and peers who uplift you.

- **Develop Self-Awareness:** Reflect on your strengths and weaknesses, leveraging both for growth.
- **Seek and Act on Feedback:** Constructive feedback is a powerful tool for improvement.
- **Embrace Continuous Learning:** Stay updated and intentional about skill development.
- **Celebrate Small Wins:** Acknowledge every achievement to boost morale and motivation.
- **Stand Up Against Bias:** Advocate for yourself and others, addressing bias calmly and constructively.
- **Be Persistent:** Resilience is built over time and through consistent practice.

The Double-Edged Sword of Resilience

Resilience often comes naturally to women, forged by lived experiences and the necessity to navigate systemic challenges. However, overusing resilience can lead to burnout and self-neglect. Balancing resilience with self-care is critical. Standing strong is important, but so is prioritizing your mental and physical health.

■ ■ ■

Well, that's a mic-drop moment if I've ever seen one. Honestly, what more could I possibly add to these incredible stories and the deep wisdom shared by these fierce Shewolves? I'm so grateful they chose to share their journeys with us—because through their stories, we learn, we grow, and we connect. Now, imagine if they hadn't shared. Imagine if anyone you've ever drawn wisdom from had decided to stay silent, for whatever reason. Think about how much we would miss—how our capacity for empathy and deep human connection would shrink. That's the power of stories. They bridge the gaps between us, remind us we're not alone, and give us the courage to rise.

Because here's the thing: They're not just telling stories. They're leaving a legacy. They know that when we put our stories into the world—when we own them, share them, and pass them down—they don't just stay with us. They ripple out. They take root in the hearts of others. They shape the next generation. Today's baby Shewolves, learning to find their voices, their strength, and their place in the world, will grow into bold, fearless, resilient mother Shewolves because of the courage of those who came before them.

Stories aren't just words on a page. They are the heartbeat of culture. They hold our values, our struggles, our hopes, and our dreams. They remind us where we've been, who we are, and what we are capable of becoming. Stories shape history. They build connection. They give us the language to name our experiences and the courage to step fully into our power.

And here's the most important part: If you don't tell your story, someone else might. And when they do, they'll shape it through their own lens, their own assumptions. But when *you* tell it—when you claim it, when you own every messy, beautiful, hard-earned truth—it becomes *yours*. And that? That is the most powerful thing we can do.

And if that's not the perfect segue into the next chapter, I don't know what is. See you there!

Chapter Recap

- Resilience isn't just a personal skill—it's a legacy, often rooted in the wisdom passed down from strong women before us, and a gift we nurture for those who come after.

- Sometimes, the Bias Monster isn't out there—it's inside us. And other times, it's woven into the very systems we navigate, daring us to confront and challenge them.

- Biases—especially the ones we hold against ourselves—can chip away at our confidence. But facing them head-on is where true personal and professional growth begins.

Embracing the Journey

Reconnecting with our intrinsic, wild woman nature is an act of self-love and resilience. And where can you rediscover that nature? In nature itself, of course. Step outside today and immerse yourself in the world around you. Feel the warmth of the sun or embrace the cleansing touch of the rain. Let nature strip away every external pressure that doesn't belong to you, so your true, untamed essence can shine through.

Chapter 6

Tell Your Story, or Someone Else Will

A compelling story is not just about what you say, but how it makes people feel.

—Miri Rodriguez

Up until now, Izzy and I have been trading off chapters in this book. It made sense—divide and conquer. Plus, we thought it would add a little extra fun for you, our readers. A little back-and-forth, a little variety. But when it came to this chapter, I knew I had to switch things up. As the resident storyteller—the one who spends her life digging into the power of stories, how they shape us, how they connect us—this one felt like mine to hold.

So here we are, back together again. And let's be honest—life's always a little more interesting when there's a few surprises along the way.

Let me just start by acknowledging the obvious: I quoted myself at the beginning of the chapter. I know, I know—it feels a little self-indulgent. But here's the thing: when the crown fits, you wear it. And storytelling? That's my crown.

When I first arrived in the United States at 13, I was hit with a tidal wave of change. New culture, new customs, and—perhaps the most overwhelming—a new language. You might think that learning a language at that age is pretty easy, especially when you're surrounded by it every day at school. And, sure, that's partly true. But let me tell you, it wasn't as simple as it sounds. Not only was this long before we had tools like Duolingo to make it easier, but I also found myself immersed in a melting pot of dialects, accents, and even other languages, both in my ESL (English as a Second Language) classes and out in the world around me. That's Miami for you—a city that proudly reflects a mix of more than 130 countries.[1] It even has its own unique English accent, affectionately known as "Miami English," or as we locals like to call it, "Mayamero."

So, imagine little old me, sitting there and listening to all these different "Englishes"—from classmates, neighbors, and even teachers! My job, it seemed, was to figure out which version was the "proper" one, which was the official way to pronounce a single word. As my brain worked its neuro-path magic, trying to make sense of it all, I slowly started to understand more and more. The thing is—I could understand way more than I could actually say. I'd hear a word, recognize all the different ways it was being used—still not entirely sure which one was technically correct—but at least I was grasping the meaning. The problem? When it came time to respond, my brain would just freeze. The words were in there somewhere, but they weren't making their way out fast enough. It was like knowing the lyrics to a song but completely blanking when it was my turn to sing.

I don't know if other bilinguals or even linguists have experienced something similar, but as my brain cracked open to this new language, I was struck by that frustrating gap. In my head, I understood so much, but I couldn't engage in conversations the way I wanted to. The words felt stuck—caught between my thoughts and my tongue. And let me tell you, nothing was more disheartening than those moments when I finally worked up the courage to respond to someone. I'd be listening to a conversation, translating what I heard from Spanish to English in my head, and just as I was about to speak—bam—someone else would jump in, cutting me off or guessing what I was going to say. The moment would pass, and there I was, left voiceless again. It wasn't just frustrating—it felt like I was being robbed of my chance to connect, to share, to truly be a part of the conversation.

Unfortunately, this story has played on repeat more times than I'd like to admit throughout my career in tech. Not because I didn't speak the language—I learned that part. But because I didn't speak *male*. Time and again, I've found myself in conversations where men would cut in, interrupt, or—my personal favorite—take my words, rephrase them, and present them as their own, as if somehow they had magically improved upon my original thought. And guess what? There's a name for this phenomenon. *Mansplaining*.

It's the art—and the audacity—of explaining something to someone who already understands it, often because *she* was the one who just explained it in the first place. And right now, I know a lot of women reading this just let out a collective sigh, because unfortunately, many of us have been there.

If you've ever been on the receiving end of mansplaining, you know just how disorienting it can be. It sneaks up on you. One moment, you're confidently speaking your truth, and the next, you're left blinking in frustration—wondering how, exactly, your own words just got hijacked and handed back to you like a gift you never asked for. It's not just annoying; it's *infuriating*. Because this isn't just about being interrupted. It's about being dismissed. It's about someone reaching in, taking your voice, and leaving you holding an empty space where your words should have been. And after 20 years in the tech industry, after experiencing this more times than I can count, I finally understood why it feels so awful.

Because it *is* awful. It *is* violating. It chips away at confidence, at credibility, at the very foundation of what it means to have a voice in the room. And that? That is something worth naming.

To clarify, I'm not talking about a moment when a friend, colleague, or well-meaning human jumps in with excitement into a conversation, eager to contribute or offer a different perspective. There's nuance here. Conversations are messy. Human connection is beautifully imperfect. And most of the time, interruptions aren't meant to silence—they come from enthusiasm, from engagement, from a desire to build on what's being said.

But then there are the moments when it's *different*. When the interruption isn't about collaboration—it's about control. When someone talks over you, not with you. When your ideas aren't expanded upon but repackaged, claimed, or dismissed entirely. And in those moments, something shifts. You *feel* it. That tiny flicker of self-doubt sneaks in. *Did I not say that clearly enough? Did I not sound confident enough? Should I just let it go?*

And this is where we find ourselves at a crossroads. Because we *do* have a choice. We can shrink back, make ourselves small, and let the moment pass. Or we can reclaim our voice—not just for ourselves, but for every woman who has ever been talked over, dismissed, or made to feel like her words didn't carry weight.

But how?

If I'm being honest, there's no magic formula, no one-size-fits-all solution for reclaiming your voice. It's personal. It's vulnerable. It's a journey that looks different for everyone. But there's one tool that has completely changed the way I approach these moments: *storytelling*.

I come from a long line of evangelical Christian pastors, and if there's one thing pastors know how to do, it's tell a *damn good* story. I grew up watching how a well-told story could move people—how it could inspire, challenge, and connect in ways that facts and figures never could. I saw how a single story, shared with conviction, could instantly change the energy in a room.

And later, when I found myself in those all-too-familiar mansplaining moments, I had a realization: If I didn't learn to craft and *courageously tell my own stories*, someone else—likely someone less qualified—would tell them for me. And they wouldn't just tell them *for* me; they'd tell them *about* me. They'd shape the narrative in ways that didn't reflect the truth of my experience, my ideas, or my worth.

Stories are our secret weapon. They're the place where we get to quiet the noise, take up space, and own the moment. They give us the power to articulate our truth, our experiences, and our hard-earned wisdom in a way that no one else can. And let's be real—it's both exhilarating and *terrifying*.

I know so many women—myself included—who would rather avoid the spotlight altogether. It feels safer to stay in the background, to let our work speak for itself, to sidestep the discomfort that comes with being truly *seen*. But here's the problem: when we step back, when we silence ourselves, we unintentionally hand over the mic to those who interrupt, dismiss, or overshadow us. And the truth is, the world *needs* your story—*not* the watered-down, secondhand version someone else tells on your behalf.

Crafting your origin story—*the* story of who you are—is like holding up a mirror to your soul. It forces you to confront the stories you've internalized, the lies you've believed, and the truths you've been too afraid to claim. And then—when you finally put it into words—you have to take the next, hardest step: stepping forward, opening a metaphorical window, and letting the world see you. It's one thing to own your story in private, but true courage comes from sharing it—letting fresh air and light pour in, exposing both the beauty and the vulnerability.

I've met so many women who want to share their stories, build their brands, or just show up authentically in the world—but the thought of crafting the perfect LinkedIn profile or curating an Instagram grid sends them spiraling into anxiety. However, that's not the point. You don't have to package your story to fit into someone else's mold. You get to decide how, where, and whom you want to share it with. You get to choose your audience. It doesn't have to be an audience of millions of people—but you do have to ask yourself, *Who needs to hear this? Who can this story serve?* As Izzy says, "You don't have to be on a stage to be or feel great about yourself." Greatness isn't about being seen by the whole world—it's about you starting to see yourself for how amazing you are and owning that story.

If there's someone who embodies this storytelling truth with effortless grace, it's Shakena Beeman, Senior Program Manager Azure Edge & Platform Engineering.

The Path to Acceptance

In 2015, when I joined Microsoft, I worked hard to convince myself that I belonged. I had the qualifications and experience to excel as a Premier Field Engineer, but I still struggled with feeling out of place. Over time, I got comfortable, the conversations flowed, and then it started happening. Almost every person I met asked me one of three questions: *What do you plan on doing next? What area are you a subject matter expert in? What is your brand?*

I worked hard to craft polished answers to these questions, but none of them felt genuine. None of them truly represented who I was or the journey that brought me to this point. I realized I was hiding parts of myself—the very parts that make me who I am today. The problem was that, even with this realization, I did little to change. I was operating in fear: fear of judgment, fear of being seen as an imposter by my peers and managers. I worried about whether I would be accepted if I showed them my true self. Would they see the value in the experiences that shaped me?

Life has a funny way of forcing you to confront the truth. In 2019, I was diagnosed with breast cancer—a diagnosis that shocked both me and my doctors, as there was no family history. That year, I underwent my first surgery, a double mastectomy, and began the reconstruction process. Then COVID-19 happened. I kept my diagnosis a secret, sharing only with a select few to justify missed work while avoiding what I feared would be negative judgment.

As the years passed, I began to share my diagnosis with colleagues and shifted my internal dialogue. It was healing. I no longer viewed my diagnosis as a burden but as a turning point—a freeing experience that brought my life into focus. It helped me embrace my past and reminded me to live fully as my authentic self. Now, I no longer omit personal aspects of my life from my professional identity, hesitate to mention my children, or downplay the journey that brought me here. Everything I have experienced makes me who I am today.

Let me tell you who I am:

I Am a Wife

My husband and I have been married for 20 years. Our partnership has taught me what it means to support and uplift someone through life's highs and lows. Together, we've faced challenges, celebrated successes, and grown both individually and as a team. While the load hasn't always been equal, we've found balance through communication, connectedness, and mindfulness.

The skills I've learned in my marriage—adaptability, support, and teamwork—are skills I bring to every role I've held. They enable me to be a collaborative teammate, an encouraging mentor, and a curious mentee. I strive to create an environment where others feel supported, whether it's helping colleagues find balance, pursue professional goals, or take care of personal matters.

I Am a Mom of Three

Being a mom to three very different boys has been both humbling and empowering. Children have no filter, and what matters to them in the moment feels like the most important thing in the world. My husband and I didn't take a one-size-fits-all approach to parenting; we adapted our style to fit each child's unique needs. Along the way, we celebrated wins, learned from mistakes, and sought advice when needed.

Motherhood has brought me immense joy and taught me about unconditional love, true acceptance, and the importance of creating inclusive environments. These lessons guide me in fostering individuality and shared success in every team I lead or work with.

I Am a Veteran

I served 10 years in the United States Air Force, where I learned about sacrifice, attention to detail, and teamwork. It was in the Air Force that I began my career in IT—as a Supply Systems Analyst and later as a Computer Systems Operator. Each role required me to not only identify problems but to always propose solutions.

The Air Force's core values—Integrity First, Service Before Self, and Excellence in All We Do—are principles I carry with me to this day. They provide the foundation for my personal and professional life.

I Am a Product of a Single-Parent Home

At 12, my parents separated, and my life was upended. My mother and I moved from Florida to Washington State, leaving behind my brother and the family I had known since birth. The following year, my sister was born, my grandfather passed away, and my world was in upheaval.

Starting over taught me resilience. I made lifelong friendships and developed the adaptability that has helped me navigate the ever-evolving world of IT.

I Am a Caretaker

From 14, I watched my mother battle various illnesses while still showing me unconditional love and fighting to enjoy the healthy moments. When I was 25, she suffered a massive stroke, and I became her caretaker while also becoming a legal guardian for my 12-year-old sister. Those years were challenging, but they shaped my ability to adapt and showed me the power of community.

That resilience was my motivation during my own medical journey. Today, I am proud to say I am a breast cancer survivor!

I Am a College Graduate

While serving in the Air Force, I earned my Associate's and Bachelor's degrees—both while pregnant with my first and second sons. Later, as a mom of three, I went back to school and earned two master's degrees: an MBA in Project Management and an MS in Information Systems. Juggling work, family, and education taught me time management and prioritization—skills I use every day.

I Am a Community Advocate

I have always been passionate about giving back. In the military, I supported employee morale and community partnerships. At Microsoft, I've taken on leadership roles in Employee Resource Groups (ERGs), serving as the time zone lead for my organization's Women's Group and Chief of Staff for the local Blacks at Microsoft ERG. Mentoring others and being mentored myself has shown me the power of representation and the importance of reaching back to lift others up. This is one of the guiding principles for my life and led me to create a non-profit, Beacon of Growth. Beacon of Growth provides support for youth ages 12–18 dealing with parents or guardians who are living with and managing chronic or severe illnesses. We aim to offer them the guidance to transition to life after high school through mentoring and scholarship opportunities.

I Am a God-Fearing Christian

Faith has guided me through life's challenges. From joining the Air Force after a chance conversation to being blessed with children despite medical odds, I've seen how God's plan has shaped my journey. Even when life didn't go according to society's definition of perfect, I've come to understand that every experience—good or bad—has made me who I am.

With newfound confidence in my journey, I am proud to introduce myself,

> I am a wife of 20 years, a mom of three incredible young men (20, 17, and 15) and a breast cancer survivor. I am the founder of Beacon of Growth Non-Profit Corporation, a God-fearing Air Force Veteran, and a Senior Program Manager at Microsoft with more than 27 years of experience in the IT industry. I am a servant leader, dedicated to creating collaborative environments where everyone feels seen and heard. I believe in paying it forward, serving the underrepresented, and showing others what's possible.

Welcome to my journey, and welcome to this beautiful adventure called life! I am Shakena Beeman!

■ ■ ■

What a beautiful way to introduce yourself, Shakena—through the power of your story. It's such a practical yet profound way to demonstrate for our readers how emotional connection happens when words are crafted with intention, care, and honesty. You've brilliantly placed yourself in front of that open window, fully exposed yet deeply relatable.

I'll admit, I wasn't nearly as eloquent as Shakena when I first began sharing my origin story. In fact, I struggled to even figure out where to start or which stories mattered enough to tell. Should I talk about the time I convinced my sister to ride a wild horse without a saddle when I was just nine years old? Or would anyone care if I admitted that I'm completely and irrationally terrified of frogs? Would anyone care about anything I had to say at all? And, honestly, *why would they?*

But here's the thing—stories like Shakena's bring forth a fundamental truth: storytelling is what makes us human. It's in our stories that we connect, empathize, and learn from one another. Stories expose the ways we're different while revealing the emotions and experiences that make us so much alike. They are the bridge that allows us to understand each other—beyond gender, beyond skin color, beyond all the labels that divide us. What a powerful antidote to racism and discrimination, to all the forces that seek to separate us.

So, where did I start with my own story? At the beginning. Simple as that. Stay with me until the end of this chapter, and I'll share a practical exercise to help you craft your own origin story. But first, let's hear from Anne-Claire (AC) Lo Bianco, Senior Partner and Program Development Manager, Microsoft for Startups, who shared some very relatable nerves when I asked her to contribute to this chapter.

Stories Connect Us All

I often find myself asking: *Why me?* Why am I working at Microsoft, the biggest tech company in the world?

And why should I be one of the women showcased in this book? It's extremely scary to put myself out there, but here I am.

My name is Anne-Claire Lo Bianco. I'm 36 years old and from a small city in northern France called Compiègne. I have a wonderful family: supportive parents, an inspiring sister, and a very talented niece. I'm French, and for the past 11 years, I've been living in London. Moving to London was a huge step for me—it was my first time studying and living abroad, and I felt so proud of myself for taking that leap. For me, it was a real achievement.

On the personal side, I'm single, have no kids, and two years ago, I ended a 12-year relationship. While this chapter is meant to focus on my professional journey, I've also been on a parallel path of learning to love my past, craft my own new narrative, and find joy in my personal growth. If someone had told me years ago that I'd one day be a Senior Program Development Manager at Microsoft, I would've laughed. Why? Because nothing in my background suggested I'd end up here. I studied Literature and History, earned a master's degree in International Business Management (and Branding—very important, LOL), but I had no technical background when I applied for my first role at Microsoft six years ago.

Loving My Past, Crafting My Narrative, and Finding Joy in Growth

But then, reflecting on my journey, I've come to understand the importance of embracing every chapter of life. Loving your past means acknowledging the triumphs and the challenges. Crafting your narrative is about taking ownership of your story. From my early career in events and marketing at the French Chamber of Great Britain to my current role at Microsoft for Startups, every experience has shaped who I am today. And when I look even beyond, I realize that I got this entrepreneurship passion and drive from my parents, who owned a company for 20 years that my grandfather built when he left Morocco for France and created a new life for his family. But one day, my parents had to close it down. I was young at that time and never understood why they were working so hard all the time, and how they managed to get back on their feet. Closing it down, closing this chapter of their life was painful. One thing I learned from it many years later from founders is that closing a startup or a chapter of your life is not a failure, it is a lesson. So yes, I am embracing the long hours, the sacrifices, the self-doubt—so much self-doubt—and I recognize how these moments taught me resilience, adaptability, and the value of continuous learning. Along the way, I've had the privilege of launching a Luxury Think Tank with inspiring leaders, as well as organizing Corporate-Startup access events with colleagues who have become lifelong friends.

At the French Chamber, I led one of the most vibrant Franco-British business communities in London, executing prestigious events such as Annual Luxury Dinners, Tech Conferences, Women & Entrepreneur Talks, and Gala Dinners. Planning events at this scale is no small feat—seating preferences, last-minute changes, deck presentations, name cards—it's chaos! If you've ever worked on something like this, you know. But none of it would have been possible without an incredible team. My point here is simple: you also don't craft your narrative alone. You lead, you support, but you're part of others' stories, and they are part of yours.

When I look back at my career at Microsoft, this lesson becomes even more profound. I started in 2018 as a vendor in the role of Community & VC Manager. I didn't have a technical background, didn't know much about venture capital, and frankly had to Bing "VC" to prepare for my interview! But I observed, I listened, I took advice, and I got to work.

I built a VC community in London, attended events, and even completed an Angel Investing course, where I met incredible people who are reshaping the way VCs invest, especially in underrepresented founders. And now, here I am—still learning, still growing, and supporting early-stage founders and students as they build their solutions on Azure.

This is what Microsoft calls a growth mindset: the belief that anyone can learn, improve, and dream big.

Finding Joy in Growth

For me, finding joy comes from professional achievements, personal development, and community involvement. I'm deeply committed to supporting underrepresented communities, whether by advocating, learning, educating, or marching. I'm proud to work for a company that values diversity, equity, and inclusion, and actively supports communities like Women and LGBTQ+IA at Microsoft.

One of my proudest accomplishments at Microsoft (and they are so many) has been to collaborate with the Playfair Capital Female Founders Office Hours initiative. Created by the Playfair Capital team in 2019, it's now the largest diversity and inclusion initiative in venture in Europe and led by the amazing Clare Zhang. It's brought together more than 2,500 female founders for 10,000 one-on-one mentoring and pitch meetings with more than 200 investors. This initiative not only represents the perfect blend of my personal passion and professional expertise, but it also allows me to work with other incredible women at Microsoft, Lora Anis-Hanna and Tiffany Johnson, who share the same commitment in championing women founders. (Yes, working at Microsoft is incredible and it enables you to achieve more!)

Acknowledging Others

Looking back, I'm grateful to the many people at Microsoft who believed in me, my passion for underrepresented founders, and for continuing to give me strength along the way. Sometimes we learn the true impact of our work through the narratives of others.

In Summary

Today, I'm loving my past as much as I can, crafting my narrative because I must, and finding joy in both my personal and professional journeys. Let's celebrate our stories—and empower others to embrace theirs

■ ■ ■

Let's do this, Anne-Claire—I'm right here with you! As I promised earlier in the chapter, I want to help you embrace your past, own your narrative, and find joy in exactly where you are right now. To do that, I'd like to share a personal exercise I created back when I found myself standing in front of that metaphorical open window. In that moment, my heart felt completely exposed—raw and vulnerable. But deep down, I knew that this very vulnerability wasn't a weakness; it was a superpower. If I leaned into it, if I chose to embrace it, I could transform both my career and my life. And so can you. Let's dive in.

Activity: Craft Your Origin Story

Warning: This activity is simple, but it is *not* easy. It's an introspective journey, a kind of time machine, that takes you back to the moments that shaped you. It's about taking ownership of your narrative, and sometimes, rewriting it entirely to make it your own.

When I first created my origin story, it took me days, maybe weeks. I still revisit it from time to time, and each time I do, I see those moments with fresh eyes. The story hasn't changed—but I have. That's the beauty of this exercise. It evolves as you do, reflecting how your experiences—and your perspective—continue to grow.

For a challenge, I once pushed myself to step outside the box by crafting my story not with words, but with numbers and symbols.

It helped me think differently about my experiences. Feel free to adapt this however it serves you best.

Steps to Crafting Your Origin Story

Start with a blank page. For extra space and creative freedom, try using large easel paper that you can stick to the wall. Be prepared to use more than one sheet—your story may need room to expand!

1. Orient the page horizontally.
2. Mark the starting point. Draw a dot on the far-left edge of the paper, about halfway down the page. This represents your birth. Write your birthdate next to it, and perhaps a symbol or icon to illustrate what this moment meant to you.
3. Add your key moments. Begin marking dots and adding icons or dates along the timeline to represent memories, people, experiences, smells, scenes—anything that you remember for some reason. Start with your earliest memories and work your way to the present.
4. Plot highs and lows. To reflect whether an experience was positive or negative, place the dot higher or lower than the invisible middle line, similar to a heartbeat graph.
5. Take your time. Add as many dots and pages as you need. This exercise might take hours, days, or even longer—give yourself the space to move at your own pace.
6. Look for patterns. As you fill in your story, you may notice recurring cycles or connections between different moments. Take note of these patterns—they're valuable insights into your journey.
7. Reflect and refine. Once your timeline is complete, revisit it. Decide which parts you want to keep private, which parts you

want to rewrite with your current understanding, and which parts you may feel ready to share with others.

This exercise isn't just about mapping your story; it's about owning it. It's a process that can help you better understand who you are and how you've become that person. And when you're ready, it's a foundation for sharing your story with the world—on your terms.

Take your time. Be kind to yourself. And remember, vulnerability is your strength—it's the heartbeat of your story.

At the start of this chapter, I mentioned that a compelling story isn't just about what you say—it's about how it makes people feel. And the most important person in that room, the one who needs to feel the story the most, is *you*. Before you share your story with others, make sure it feels empowering, inspiring, and true to you. It doesn't have to be perfect—in fact, it *shouldn't* be. The She of this world? We laugh in the face of perfectionism! Come along to the next chapter and see exactly how we do it!

Chapter Recap

- Through storytelling, you can take back control of your personal story, amplify your voice, and create meaningful connections with others.

- A compelling story is about how it makes people feel, and the most important person who needs to connect with it is *you*. Owning your narrative gives you the power to shape how the world sees you, rather than letting others define it for you.

- Crafting your origin story is an empowering exercise to help you embrace your past, identify key life patterns, and decide how to share your experiences authentically.

Embracing the Journey

Rewriting pieces of your origin story is a bold act of courage. It's declaring to the world—and to yourself—that *you* are the author of your life. It's taking those moments when someone labeled you, cast you into a system, or told you "no," and transforming them into stepping stones toward something bigger and better for your destiny. Be courageous. Be a storyteller. Own your narrative and let your story roar.

Chapter 7

Let's Laugh at Perfectionism

Perfectionism is self-abuse of the highest order.
—Anne Wilson Schaef

There was a time at Microsoft, many years ago, when perfectionism wasn't just present—it was quietly celebrated and even rewarded. Of course, no one called it "perfectionism," but the unspoken expectation was clear: going above and beyond was the baseline standard. That pressure permeated the culture, creating competition and, at times, division among colleagues.

What's more, it placed relentless pressure on people to be flawless in all aspects of their work. And let's be honest, isn't that a burden women have carried for generations? Striving for perfection feels almost ingrained in us—woven into the fabric of what society expects. As *Psychology Today* aptly puts it, perfectionism is "a trait that makes life an endless report card on accomplishments or looks."

Microsoft called it "Calibration."

I call it bullshit.

The truth is, the pursuit of perfection, especially for women, is not new. Across cultures and history, women have been held to impossible standards. Just look at history: in Asia, women endured the painful process of foot-binding to achieve smaller feet—an excruciating practice that involved breaking the arch and curling the toes under, often causing lifelong health issues. In Europe, women teetered under the weight of elaborate wigs, so large and heavy they sometimes caused them to lose their balance. These wigs—crafted from horsehair, human hair, and even wool—were status symbols, but they were also absurdly uncomfortable. And let's not even get started on today's beauty standards—we'd be here all day.

The relentless pursuit of perfection is both exhausting and unattainable. And the irony is that deep down, we know it doesn't even exist! Yet we keep chasing it, and worse, we pull everyone around us into the race. We strive for every moment, every task, every part of life to be flawless at all times. Has anyone ever encountered such a miracle? I doubt it.

Thankfully, for many of us, we finally realize that this ideal is simply absurd. It happens in our own time and space, but it's when we come to that realization, we begin to lead simpler, more meaningful, and more authentic lives, letting go of impossible standards. Then when we start to project this understanding onto those around us—our families, our friends, our colleagues—it can create a ripple effect. It frees others, too.

When I look back now, I can even laugh at my own perfectionist tendencies. I was part of that group of people of "everything must be perfect, or it's not worth doing." It was a hard way to live. Letting go of perfectionism didn't suddenly make life easy, but it did make life more balanced. I learned that chasing perfection often means sacrificing something else—your time, your energy, your relationships. Letting go of it opened space for growth, reflection, and more realistic expectations of myself and others.

This chapter delves into the stories of the perfectly imperfect women at Microsoft who have grappled with perfectionism—embracing it, battling it, stumbling through it, and ultimately discovering freedom in imperfection. The She reminds us that perfection isn't a requirement for effectiveness. In fact, it's often our imperfections that lead to more authentic, creative, and impactful results.

And maybe, just maybe, the real power isn't just in breaking free from it—but in standing tall, smiling, and daring to laugh right in its face.

 "Just. Press. Send." by Oksana Maleshykhina, Senior Technical Specialist

I still cringe when I remember the day my child came home from school, beaming with pride and announcing, "I got 98% on my science test, the highest in my grade!" And my first reaction? "What happened to the other 2%?" I even grunted, "You can't build a bridge at 98%. It's either built or not."

Hi, I'm Oksana. By day, I connect with customers to inspire them and bring order to chaos. For years, I believed perfectionism was my superpower. Everything I did had to be flawless—or it wasn't worth doing. I expected 100% from myself and, if I'm honest, I projected that expectation onto everyone around me, too. At work, I allowed for the idea that "not everyone is perfect," but at home, I had a very different standard.

Looking back, I can laugh at my past self—and trust me, laughing has been essential in this journey. Now, I deliberately celebrate achievements first. Then, with curiosity (and far less pressure), I might ask about that "missing 2%"—if it even matters at all. No more talks about theoretical bridges.

That relentless pursuit of perfection followed me into my professional life, where I treated perfection as the gold standard for everything I touched. But then I stepped into a Technical Program Manager role at Microsoft Engineering, and the sheer pace of change flipped my world upside down. With an ever-growing workload, tasks spanning multiple time zones, and weekly interactions with hundreds of people, I quickly spiraled into stress and exhaustion—both self-inflicted. Perfectionism was dragging me down, not lifting me up.

The turning point came during the pandemic. The world went into lockdown, and with everyone at home, my work in Teams Engineering skyrocketed as demand surged. At the same time, I had to manage homeschooling, three meals a day, house chores, and the delicate task of maintaining peace and harmony at home.

Perfection? Forget it. Life was no longer about building a flawless bridge. It became a winding path full of unexpected twists, where "good enough" had to be the goal. And let me tell you, shifting from my perfectionist mindset to a "reasonable" one was not easy. My so-called superpower became a burden I needed to shed.

That's when it hit me—perfectionism isn't perfect. In fact, it's often the opposite. For so long, I had carried cultural and personal expectations to be the perfect daughter, wife, mother, and employee. Growing up, I was taught to focus on fixing weaknesses and making everything flawless. But when I moved to another country, I observed something liberating: people celebrated their strengths and let the rest be "okay-ish." It was a revelation—and it made so much sense.

Still, I struggled to let go. My academic background in mathematics, where precision is king, didn't help. Math is black and white, with clear right and wrong answers. But life isn't an equation. Life is messy, variable, and wonderfully unpredictable. I needed to stop treating it like a math problem to solve.

Now, don't get me wrong—I'm still on this journey. I don't want to abandon all my perfectionist tendencies; they have their place. But I've learned that some perfectionist habits need to go. For example, I used to spend ages reviewing and rewriting even simple messages. Now, I use the 20–80 rule: only 20% of emails and chats need to be perfect. The rest? They just need to get the point across. Most of the time, it's in the 80%. *Just press send.*

Some things, though, I still make perfect—like birthday cakes. My version of perfect, anyway.

The biggest lesson I've learned is to embrace and laugh at my imperfections. Laughing has been a life-changer for me and my family. Perfectionism, I now understand, is a double-edged sword. Striving for excellence is valuable, but demanding perfection in every aspect of life is exhausting and counterproductive. Not everything needs to be perfect to be effective.

By letting go of perfectionism, I've found a balance that works for me. So here's to progression, not perfection—and to finding joy in the perfectly imperfect journey of life. Just. Press. Send. And maybe, take a moment to laugh along the way.

■ ■ ■

Oksana's story brought me back to my own quiet reflections during COVID-19—a time marked by so much loss, but also by the hope that we might gain something deeper in the process. The pandemic became one of the busiest periods of my life. I was working tirelessly to help clients transition to Teams—not as an exciting new innovation, but as the only way to keep their businesses alive.

But amid the chaos, something unexpected happened. I began to experience deeper connections with people. I found myself talking with people not just about work, but about life, family, and what really mattered. I remember sitting in my son's room late at night, leaning against the wall during calls because my home office doubled as our bedroom, and the rest of my family was already asleep. My days were carved into two brief hours with my family, followed by calls that stretched long into the night. During this time, perfectly tailored suits were replaced by sweats, with kids running around and dogs barking. Nothing was perfect, but at the same time everything was making perfect sense. I redefined how I showed up—not through makeup or a perfectly tailored dress, but through my competence and the ability to guide my customers with clarity and confidence. This experience wasn't just about solving business challenges; it became about building deeper, more human connections.

For a time, it felt like we were all part of a cultural shift. People started to rethink what work-life balance really meant. They held their family closer, fiercely protected the time they carved out for themselves, and many weren't willing to let go of those changes. But as the world reopened, the old pressures quietly crept back in. Companies pushed for a return to familiar routines, and before long, the relentless pace resumed. The lessons of the pandemic—though deeply felt—began to fade as the world tried to move forward as if nothing had changed.

A crisis like the pandemic can serve as a wake-up call. It pushes us to embrace imperfection, to reevaluate what truly matters. But sometimes, it's not the crisis—it's the grind itself that pushes us to reckon with our choices. For Jennifer, that "grind" became the beginning of something entirely new.

"CEO of My Life" by Jennifer Cooper, Former Microsoft DEI Leader and Chief of Staff

I hate role-playing. You know the drill—the classic classroom tactic where "volunteers" are thrust into a made-up scenario and expected to act out what they'd do. Everyone pretends it's real, but my brain can't help but dissect the setup, obsess over the "right" answer, and brace for the inevitable embarrassment when I fail to nail it. Role-playing is like a lose-lose riddle, and when you don't hit the mark, everyone pretends it doesn't sting. But it does. At least for me.

There I was, sitting in an all-day leadership and management workshop at Microsoft, surrounded by actual leaders. But I wasn't one of them. As an individual contributor with no team to manage, I felt out of place in that very corporate (and very beige) conference room in Building 92 at Microsoft headquarters. I took a few notes, but my mind was elsewhere—buzzing with a call from my realtor, looming divorce paperwork, a pending mortgage for a house I'd be buying on my own, all while raising three little humans. Life wasn't just busy; it was overwhelming, chaotic, and undeniably messy.

Then came the dreaded announcement: a role-playing exercise. I groaned, probably out loud. Kim, the instructor, handed me a piece of paper and congratulated me on landing the "CEO role." *Oh, great. Just what I needed—a crash course in pretending to be someone I wasn't while trying to focus on real-life challenges.* "Welcome to the executive lounge," she said with a smile, pointing me to a beige couch outside the beige room. My co-CEO kicked back, clearly coasting through the simulation. I sat there stewing.

The timer buzzed, and we shuffled through rounds of simulations, debriefs, and escalating confusion. Workers debated privacy, managers were stuck on compensation, and senior leaders were fretting over data breaches. Meanwhile, my co-CEO joked about how "easy" it was to be the boss. I couldn't take it anymore.

That's when it happened—my *aha!* moment. Desperate to end the chaos and regain some sense of myself, I broke the rules. As CEO, I was supposed to stay in the lounge and only interact with senior leaders when summoned. But I was done. I walked straight into the room, ignoring any protests (including the one from my inner rule-follower), and surveyed the situation. Workers huddled in whispers, managers stood by looking defeated, and senior leaders peppered me with a barrage of questions.

"Enough," I thought. "Everyone, sit down and talk to me." My brain screamed, *YOU'RE BREAKING THE RULES!* But I didn't care. I read aloud the instructions on my CEO paper, asking people to share what they needed and what was holding them back. Within minutes, everyone pulled up chairs, shared information, and, for the first time that day, collaborated. The task was completed in record time.

The instructors walked over, stunned. Most groups never finish this task, they explained—let alone do it by breaking the rules. I wasn't a manager or a CEO. Heck, I wasn't even supposed to be in that room. But by leaning into my authenticity—empathy and humility instead of scripted authority—I got it done.

That moment taught me something powerful: sometimes, breaking the rules is exactly what's needed. My strength wasn't pretending to be a CEO; it was being myself. I stopped playing the game and leaned into who I am—a person who listens, empathizes, and leads with humility.

Since that day, I've carried this lesson with me. When my inner critic tells me I don't belong in a room or at a table of leaders, I remind myself that my worth isn't tied to a title. My authenticity and strengths are what make me worthy.

And as for role-playing? I still hate it. But now I laugh about it. Because sometimes the best thing you can do is embrace the imperfection of the moment, break a few rules, and laugh at them. So here's to authenticity—and laughing at the ridiculousness of trying to be "perfect."

■ ■ ■

Jennifer's story is such a profound truth: Our worth isn't defined by a title. And yet, I often think about the many titles—the many hats—we, as women, wear at once. With each one comes the quiet, unspoken expectation that we give 100%—not 98%—to every single role. We push ourselves to be everything to everyone, striving for perfection even in systems that rarely give us 100% in return.

In 2023, Claudia Goldin won the Nobel Prize in Economics[1] for her groundbreaking research into gender disparities in the workforce. Her findings revealed that women continue to face wage gaps and career stagnation after having children due to occupational segregation, fewer work hours due to caregiving demands, and outright discrimination. So here we are, striving for perfection in every single role we have, while the systems around us fail to support us—and, in turn, we fail ourselves by clinging to impossible standards.

Diane tells us what can happen if we decide to let go of those expectations and begin to ask ourselves: What *really* matters?

"Making My Rounding" by Diane C. Boettcher, Director of Business Management, Industry Solutions Delivery, Americas

My time in the Navy taught me a fundamental truth: not everything matters equally. In the military, life-or-death decisions are separated from trivial details with laser clarity. We had explicit labels for actions—warnings for life-threatening risks, cautions for potential harm to people or equipment, and notes for general awareness. That kind of prioritization helped me focus on what truly mattered and let go of the rest. And let me tell you, it came with a healthy dose of perspective—and humor. Not every mistake was a catastrophe. If a uniform patch was misplaced, it might earn a laugh during the next meeting, but it didn't derail the mission.

I carried those lessons with me into civilian life, but applying them hasn't always been easy. When I moved back to the United States from Singapore, it was one of the most challenging transitions of my career. After years as an M2 at Microsoft—a "manager of managers"—I was stepping into an M1 role, managing a single team. It was the right decision for my family, but it felt like a demotion. The hierarchical nature of corporate life ties worth so tightly to titles, and I couldn't shake the weight of what others might think.

During that time, I leaned heavily on my military training. In the Navy, perfection was never about never making mistakes—it was about knowing which moments demanded precision and which didn't. I often think back to the World War II practice of tying used morphine syringes to wounded soldiers' uniforms so medics wouldn't accidentally administer a fatal second dose. That level of detail was life or death. But if someone's uniform patch was crooked? That could wait for a good laugh. It was this ability to separate the critical from the trivial that helped me recalibrate my approach to perfectionism in the corporate world.

At Microsoft, I started redefining what success looked like for me. I asked myself, "What really matters?" and began focusing on purpose over perfection. My decision to take the M1 role wasn't a failure—it was a deliberate choice to prioritize my family. That clarity didn't make it easy to shake the pressure to overachieve, but it gave me a direction.

One phrase from my Navy days stuck with me: "If the minimum wasn't good enough, it wouldn't be the minimum." It was like a built-in permission slip to stop over-delivering on things that didn't really matter. I adopted a new framework I called "making my rounding," a way to evaluate if something was worth my energy. Managing a $12.5 million book of business, I realized that spending time on a $30,000 issue didn't make my rounding—it was better left to someone else.

I also began to laugh more at the ridiculousness of my own perfectionist tendencies. Like the mornings when urgent work calls interrupted my workout—forcing me to unmute, pretend I wasn't panting, and conduct business mid-run. Or worse, the times I'd jump out of the shower to answer a call, trying to sound composed while dripping water everywhere. Corporate life, like any other part of life, is messy. And honestly? The messiness is kind of hilarious.

The move back to the United States also made me confront my fears about how others might perceive me. Would they see my role change as a step backward? But then I realized that most people weren't analyzing my career trajectory as much as I thought they were. Most people are too busy dealing with their own lives to spend much time scrutinizing mine. That realization was freeing.

The biggest shift came when I stopped seeing mistakes—or what I perceived as failures—as career-ending. Instead, I started seeing them as opportunities to grow. A mentor once told me, "If you make the wrong decision, you'll find out soon enough, and then you'll make another decision." It was a beautifully simple reminder that mistakes are just part of the process.

Today, I see perfectionism for what it really is—a myth. It's not about avoiding every mistake or succeeding in every single area. It's about figuring out what truly matters, letting the rest go, and being able to laugh when life gets messy. Whether it's the chaos of corporate life or the curveballs of parenthood, I've learned that laughter and letting go are powerful antidotes to the pressure of perfection.

So here's my advice: embrace imperfection. Laugh at it. Life will never be perfect—corporate life certainly won't—but when we learn to laugh at the absurdity of striving for 100% all the time, we free ourselves to focus on what's truly important.

■ ■ ■

It's true—our relentless pursuit of perfection can blur the very things that matter most. And perhaps the hardest part isn't just what we sacrifice along the way, but who we become in the process. That's exactly what happened to Sonia. She pushed forward until she reached her breaking point, just before burnout consumed her completely.

"Passport, Please!" By Sonia Cuff, Principal Cloud Advocate Lead

"Microsoft is like a Labrador. It will eat anything you feed it—and then come back begging for more."

Mark's words stuck with me. He was the kind of person whose advice had a way of staying with you because it was always right on target. He had taken a chance on me—an 18-year-old with no formal training—and hired me into the IT department of the bank where I worked. At the time, I was the youngest person in the branch, with a grand total of three years of high school Computer Studies to my name. I'd started as a bank teller but quickly became the go-to person for all computer issues. Mark saw potential in me before I even saw it in myself.

Later, he nudged me to learn about this thing called "the cloud," long before it became the juggernaut it is today. Again, great advice. But his gentle warning about Microsoft—that it could consume everything you threw at it—hit me differently when I was thinking about applying for a role there.

Like that Labrador, I wasn't great at self-regulation either. I was eager to prove myself, to show I could do it all, and I didn't really know when—or how—I should stop. My career was built on saying yes to opportunities others believed I could handle, even when I wasn't so sure myself. I borrowed their confidence, dove in, and figured things out. That approach led me from troubleshooting to national IT projects, from green screens to Windows NT systems, and eventually into systems architecture and technical consulting.

But my desire to excel—to be perfect—started to take a toll on me. I worked tirelessly to meet every demand, always striving to do more, do better, and prove my worth. I was determined, capable, and juggling more than anyone should. And eventually, cracks started to show.

What no one saw—and what I was too proud to admit—was how much I was struggling. I was in a constant state of stress. My body couldn't relax. I couldn't fall asleep at night, and when I woke up, I was already exhausted. I carried my phone everywhere, even when stepping out of a room, and my heart raced every time it rang. Taking time off felt like torture because being disconnected only made me catastrophize about what I might be missing.

Then one day, everything came crashing down. I stood in a client's server room, listening to their plans for an upcoming outage, and had a wild, desperate thought: This isn't going to be my problem because I won't be here. That morning, I had quietly slipped my passport into my bag, fully intending to walk out of that meeting, hail a taxi to the airport, and buy a ticket on the next flight—anywhere. Without telling my boss. Without telling the client. Without telling my husband.

Burnout doesn't announce itself. It creeps in slowly, especially for people who love their jobs and are really good at them. It starts as a spark, then smolders quietly, building into a room filled with smoke. You can't see the flames, but you can feel the suffocating heat. And when your body is flooded with Cortisol, the stress hormone, it takes over. Your brain focuses on survival, and you start making, well, not the best decisions.

I laugh now that I was still dedicated enough to take that last customer meeting before planning my grand escape. But instead of calling a taxi, I found myself walking back to my office. I locked myself in a meeting room and called my husband. "I need you to pick me up," I said. "I can't do this anymore."

That moment forced me to confront the truth: my relentless pursuit of perfection had nearly driven me to the edge. I had to learn to let go of the unrealistic expectations I placed on myself and redefine what success—and balance—looked like.

Since then, I've had many demanding roles—managing millions in revenue, running our own business, raising a family, and now leading two teams at Microsoft. I've learned it is possible to recover from burnout and even thrive, but it's a constant balancing act.

I now see work-life balance as a long-term game. You can have it all—just not all at once. Some days, work takes priority, and I miss birthdays or Mother's Day. Other times, I'm at a Pilates class or completely unplugged, making memories with my family.

I've also learned to nurture parts of myself outside of work. For years, I volunteered with Emergency Services, helping during floods and cyclones and even training others. Later, when that became too much, I found new outlets—like joining a community choir, where I sing alto and get a much-needed endorphin boost.

This experience has made me better at advocating for myself—and for others. I now protect my time, set boundaries, and encourage my team to do the same. I remind them to ask not just, "Can I do this?" but, "Do I have the capacity to do this?" Everyone's limits are different, and my job is to help people find what works for them.

With the support of great mentors and some hard-earned lessons, I've learned to tame the Labrador inside. Occasionally, I still feed it too much, but I now know when to step back and recharge. I love my job, but I also know that my downtime is critical for coming back as my best self. Perfection may seem like a noble pursuit, but the truth is, sometimes the most powerful thing you can do is say no, take a breath, and just let the pup wait.

■ ■ ■

I think Sonia may have learned to transform her Labrador into a wolf—and she's running with it! I can certainly relate to her story. Like Sonia, I've struggled with the challenge of saying no throughout my career. Many of my opportunities came from saying yes—sometimes without hesitation—which conditioned me to keep saying yes, almost instinctively. Over time, it became second nature—so much so that I forgot how to say no! I know this struggle is familiar to so many women. It's one of the unintended consequences of our pursuit of perfection.

The truth is, being a chronic "yes person" isn't just about overcommitting—it's what drives burnout. It's a cycle that's all too easy to slip into and incredibly hard to break. While learning to say no—to set boundaries, to protect our time and energy—is one of the most powerful acts of self-preservation we can embrace.

In the next chapter, we'll hear from the She who didn't just come close to burnout—she faced it head-on. The women of Microsoft will share their struggles and the hard-earned lessons they've learned about keeping their passion alive—staying on fire—without burning out. Follow us to Chapter 8!

Chapter Recap

- Perfectionism often masquerades as a noble pursuit, but the truth is, it frequently leads to stress, burnout, and, most heartbreakingly, a loss of self.

- By embracing imperfection, we rediscover our authenticity and vulnerability—qualities that don't just make us more human but also more effective, creative, and fulfilled in both our work and our lives.

- Saying "yes" to every opportunity might seem like the path to success, but it can quickly turn into a destructive habit that drains your energy and leaves little room for what truly matters.

Embracing the Journey

When was the last time you laughed so hard your stomach hurt, tears streamed down your face, and you forgot all about being "perfect"? Step into the role of CEO of your own life. Listen to your inner voice. Tune out the noise of expectations trying to shape you into someone you're not. And when the pressure feels overwhelming—laugh. Laugh at the noise, laugh at yourself, and let that laughter set you free.

Chapter 8

Stay On Fire but Don't Burn Out

Breathe. Let go. And remind yourself that this very moment is the only one you know you have for sure.
—Oprah Winfrey

Fire to the Rain

It was my birthday, and I was sitting on the soccer field at Microsoft's main campus, drenched from the steady Seattle rain. The empty field, slick with water under the floodlights, felt like the loneliest place in the world. My tears mixed with the rain, streaming down my face as I sobbed uncontrollably, gasping for air between waves of frustration and exhaustion. It was well past 11 PM, and I had no way home—I'd missed the last bus. My clothes clung to me like the crushing weight of my own expectations.

The field, normally a place for camaraderie and competition, felt alien in its stillness. It seemed to mock me, as if the floodlights were exposing every crack in my resolve. I'd stayed late at work, convinced I could solve a bug that had been tormenting me for days. I told myself it would be the perfect birthday gift: finishing the task and silencing my self-doubt. "Once it's done, I'll feel better," I thought. But as the hours ticked by and the frustration mounted, I realized I'd only succeeded in pushing myself to a breaking point. Instead of giving myself a victory, I'd given myself a collapse.

This wasn't just about a bug in the code—it was about an internal bug *bugging* me to prove my worth. Early in my career at Microsoft, Imposter Syndrome had its claws deep in me. I was working on Object Linking and Embedding (OLE) in Word, a notoriously complex area that constantly challenged my confidence. The bug I couldn't fix became a metaphor for my perceived inadequacy. That night, sitting on the cold, wet turf, I hit rock bottom.

The next day, with a clearer head, I solved the problem in a fraction of the time I'd spent spinning my wheels the night before. That should have been my wake-up call, but it wasn't. The continued drive to push myself didn't vanish—it lurked in the background, waiting for the next opportunity to strike.

Fast-forward a few years, after my first maternity leave, and I found myself in a new firestorm of self-imposed pressure. I had rejoined Microsoft to work on a high-profile project: real-time typing in Word desktop. The team was full of energy, with young engineers pulling long hours and feeding off each other's excitement. It was cutting-edge work, and the executives were buzzing.

As a senior on the team, I felt I had to lead by example. I told myself I needed to match their energy, their hours, their impact—if not surpass them. I didn't want anyone to think motherhood had slowed me down. "It's fine," I told myself. "My son is already asleep when I get home, so staying late doesn't matter." Nine o'clock became my shut down norm at work.

And the second strike came. The migraines came first—ocular migraines that blurred my vision. Then the stress hit my body in other ways: I developed dandruff and found myself constantly on edge. My energy was draining, my health was deteriorating, and I felt like I was slowly unraveling. Sadly, no one seemed to notice.

One evening, I couldn't take it anymore. Desperate and overwhelmed, I sent my manager an email. I didn't have the words to fully explain my struggles, but I told him I needed a reset. I was taking all four weeks of my vacation to step away and regain my balance. He approved, but there was no recognition of the deeper issue, no support offered. I felt like a cog in the machine, easily replaced, invisible.

Rekindling the Fire with Purpose

During that break, I had time to think, to breathe, and to come back to myself. When I returned, my former manager reached out with an opportunity to lead accessibility efforts in Word. It was a project that not only shifted my career but also reshaped my approach to work.

Accessibility became the fire that reignited my purpose. It wasn't just about the technical challenges—it was about the impact. I was empowering people with disabilities, creating tools that made digital documents accessible to low-vision users using screen reading technologies. The work mattered deeply, and for the first time, I felt the fulfillment of doing something with purpose.

This time, I approached the work differently. I set boundaries. I stopped working late into the night, realizing it wasn't productive. I learned that stepping away, giving myself time to rest, often led to solutions coming naturally the next day. Sometimes I'd solve the problem in the quiet of my mind, in the background of my thoughts. Other times, someone else would find the answer—and that was okay, too.

Burnout didn't vanish overnight, but I began to recognize the signs. I started to laugh at the absurdity of perfectionism—like the mornings I took work calls during my workouts, unmuting between breaths, pretending I wasn't panting. Life wasn't perfect, and neither was I, but I was learning to be okay with that.

The Shift to Balance

The real breakthrough came when I started leaning into my strengths. Instead of chasing perfection, I focused on what truly mattered. I compartmentalized my tasks, prioritized effectively, and became intentional about how I spent my energy.

Over time, my confidence grew even more. I stopped doubting my worth, and I stopped tying it to how late I stayed or how perfect my work appeared. This shift led to a promotion into management—a role where I no longer battled Imposter Syndrome. I knew I belonged because I could see the value I brought.

One memory stands out as a testament to how far I've come. When I was pregnant with my second child, my manager offered me a promotion to lead a team. "We'll wait for you," he said, smiling at my very pregnant belly. "You're the right person for this." That moment meant everything to me. It was proof that I didn't need to burn out to prove myself, and that the right opportunities would come when I focused on what truly mattered.

Satya Nadella often says, "Do great work, and the right things will happen." For me, the right things happened not because I worked myself into the ground, but because I learned to laugh at the trap of perfectionism. I let go of the need to do it all and embraced the freedom of doing what matters most.

Lessons from the Flames

For anyone who finds themselves on the edge of burnout, here's what I've learned: Perfectionism isn't a badge of honor—it's a trap. Burnout doesn't happen overnight. It creeps up on you, whispering that you just need to work harder, stay later, do more. If you ever find yourself sobbing on a soccer field, drenched in rain and exhaustion, ask yourself if what you're chasing is really worth it. Then laugh—because it probably isn't. Step back. Breathe. And remember, you're already enough.

Closing Reflections

"Burnout isn't just exhaustion; it's the result of unregulated passion, ambition, or an overcommitted heart. The key isn't to dim your fire but to control it, channel it, and let it fuel you sustainably. Life's most fulfilling moments come not from perfection but from purpose. Tend to your fire carefully, and it will light your way to success and joy."

—Steph Burg, Principal Director of Engineering

■ ■ ■

Talk about rising from the ashes *of burnout*! Steph's story took me back to a moment when Miri and I were working on this book. There were stretches of time when I was fully immersed in the writing process—so determined to finish certain chapters that I set aside everything else and began to channel all my energy into moving the book forward. I was focused, driven—ready to push through.

But as life often does, it reminded me that I am not invincible. Out of nowhere, I started feeling unwell. My ear swelled up, and suddenly, I was caught in a literal spiral—my body forcing me to stop. The only thing left to do was listen to the doctor's orders: rest. Rest? It felt impossible. My mind was ready, my heart was ready—or at least, that's what I had believed.

Burnout is like a shadowy antagonist lurking behind the scenes. It preys on our ambition, tempting us to keep going, even when we know we shouldn't. And if we let even a single spark of it catch, it can quickly spiral into an uncontrollable blaze, consuming everything in its path—including us. It's one thing to talk about not burning out or learning lessons from the flames . . . metaphorically. But when life throws you into an actual war, "fire" takes on an entirely new and deeply personal meaning.

Wisdom Forged in Fire

Before the invasion, my life felt stable, even predictable. I'd been at Microsoft for nearly a decade, found a healthy work-life balance, and welcomed my second child after three years at the company. I was proud of my ability to juggle both my role as a mom and my career. Sure, there were occasional "fires" to manage, but nothing I couldn't handle. Then, February 24, 2022, happened. Fires turned into real flames—missiles, explosions, destroyed buildings, and lives lost.

My name is Nataliia Burlakova, Senior Specialist, and I'm a proud mom of two boys. Including my husband, that makes three boys in total—so my personal life is far less gender-diverse than my professional one! I've spent my entire career in multinational companies, and for the last 12 years, I've been at Microsoft. Before the war, being "on fire" was just a figure of speech. Since the invasion of Ukraine, staying "on fire but not burning out" has become a literal challenge.

It's hard to share this story because I wouldn't wish this experience on anyone. But I also understand now how easy and blessed my life was before. I'm sharing this to show that even in the most difficult, terrifying circumstances, it's possible to keep going—to live, to work, and to protect what matters most.

After almost three years of war, I've built a new kind of stability, one based on resilience and preparation. I've adapted to a reality no one should ever have to face. I've learned to manage my home like a survivalist: I have massive power banks to keep the refrigerator running during outages, energy-efficient lamps, and special heaters for the brutal winters. I've memorized the energy consumption of every appliance in my house to optimize its use. It's not just survival—it's a masterclass in sustainable living.

I also have two types of shelters for my family. When drone attacks threaten, we retreat to the wardrobe or bathroom, following the "two walls rule," which means placing at least two walls between us and the outside. For missile strikes, we head to the underground parking area beneath our building, as the potential damage from missiles is far greater.

The hardest moments are seeing my kids sleeping on the floor of our wardrobe or in our car in the underground parking while explosions rumble nearby. Yet, their resilience amazes me. Kids adapt so much faster than adults. One morning, on the way to school, the attack alarm went off. I froze, unsure whether to turn back or continue. My older son calmly checked the alert details on his phone. "It's missiles from strategic aviation," he said. "We have about 40 minutes. Take us to school—it'll only take 10 minutes—and then you can get home in time to shelter." At school, lessons continue even in shelters, often without electricity. My boys carry emergency backpacks every day, filled with water, food, power banks, and medicine.

As I write this in late 2024, we've endured 1,419 attack alarms totaling more than 1,650 hours in shelters. That's weeks of our lives spent hiding underground. Some attacks last 10 minutes; others stretch on for 14 hours.

Managing daily life under these circumstances is a constant logistical challenge. I have to plan everything around electricity outages: when to cook, shower, do laundry, or wash dishes. I've become an expert in the most energy-efficient modes for my appliances. Sometimes, I even adjust work meetings to fit around these windows. Thankfully, my PC doesn't consume much power, so I can continue working, even during outages.

One question I still get—one that frustrates me deeply—is, "Why don't you leave? You have kids." First, my kids don't want to leave. Ukraine is their home. Second, if everyone left, who would keep the economy running, pay taxes, volunteer, and support those on the frontlines? Who would rebuild? I still wrestle with guilt that I'm not on the battlefield, even though I know my role as a mother and a citizen is equally important.

Before the war, my favorite quote was, "What doesn't kill us makes us stronger." Not anymore. I wouldn't wish for anyone to endure what we've endured. No one should have to face death or destruction to grow stronger.

This war has redefined everything for me—my priorities, my perspective, and my resilience. It has taught me that even when the world feels like it's burning around you, you can find ways to keep going. Not perfectly, not without fear, but with strength, determination, and hope.

■ ■ ■

These stories offer powerful lessons, but what strikes me most is the deep irony at their heart: the very steps we take to survive burnout are often the same ones we need to prevent emotional and mental exhaustion in the first place.

At their core, these stories are teaching us something essential—balance. The ability to meet life's demands without losing sight of who we are. To move forward with purpose, but also with compassion—for others and for ourselves. They remind us that resilience isn't just about pushing through hardship. It's about recognizing when to pause, when to shift course, and when to trust that even in moments of stillness, we are still growing, still progressing.

In my own experience, and through the wisdom of friends and colleagues, I've discovered four brilliant and applicable truths that are helping me cultivate this balance:

1. Date Your Company, Don't Marry It

I'll never forget the first time I heard this from Miri—it was like a lightbulb went off. This isn't about being unprofessional or not caring about your work; it's about keeping a healthy relationship with your employer. Treat it like dating: keep things fresh and exciting, but don't take on the weight of every company problem as if it's your own. Remember the Labrador: A company will take as much as you're willing to give, but it's up to you to decide how much you want to give—and make sure the relationship benefits you, too. Balance is key.

2. **You Can Have It All, Just Not All at Once**

This one hits close to home. Sometimes, our ambition or perfectionism tricks us into thinking we need to do everything, all at once. But when we pile too much on our plates, our bodies and minds have a way of saying, enough. The art of balance lies in learning to prioritize—rethinking what truly matters most to you in the moment and giving it your focus. Doing a thousand things at once often leaves you burned out and unfulfilled. Instead, focus on doing fewer things well and with intention.

3. **Other People's Fears Don't Have to Be Yours**

Grounding yourself in reality is important, but don't let fear—or other people's doubts—keep you from dreaming big or taking risks. Life is short. *Carpe diem!* Some of the greatest regrets come from the things we didn't try, the love we didn't give, or the dreams we didn't chase. Surround yourself with people who believe in you. It doesn't have to be a large group—just the kind of people who make you feel bigger, braver, and bolder.

4. **Deliver Your Best Each Day**

I'll never forget something a woman said during a Microsoft webinar: "You might not be at your best today, but you can still deliver the best you have to give today." It's a simple but profound idea. Focus on being the best version of yourself each day—not perfect, but the best you can be in the moment. Celebrate small wins, be kind to yourself, and let go of harsh self-judgment. By doing so, you build a sense of accomplishment and self-worth that fuels your resilience and well-being over time.

These lessons have stayed with me because they're not just about avoiding burnout; they're about thriving in a way that feels sustainable and joyful. Such is the story of Wendy Wang, Senior Software Engineer, who draws a connection between math and music and hopes to perform in the Van Cliburn International Piano Competition someday.

The Rhythm of Balance

Coding and playing the piano may seem worlds apart, but for me, they are two sides of the same coin. Like music, coding involves following a "score" to create something meaningful—a program instead of a composition. Both require persistence, attention to detail, and a deep appreciation for the process. Whether you're crafting a melody that touches hearts or developing software used by millions, the experience is deeply rewarding.

It's this intricate interplay between logic and creativity that keeps me energized and inspired. As a software engineer at Microsoft, I spend my days developing the content platform for public-facing Microsoft sites. In the evenings, I transform into a musician, dedicating two to three hours daily to practicing the piano. Don't worry about my neighbors—I have a silent piano, so they're spared my late-night sessions!

My love for the piano began in China, where I practiced despite a demanding school schedule. At 16, I had the opportunity to study in Massachusetts as part of an exchange program, but piano lessons seemed financially out of reach. Then, a series of incredible acts of generosity changed everything. The Cape Cod Conservatory offered me a tuition discount, I won a scholarship, and someone I'd never met, John Gage, donated a piano to me. These acts of kindness allowed me to pursue my passion all the way through graduation.

But after that, life got in the way. I took a long break from piano while focusing on my career, and for a while, it felt like a void. Eventually, I realized something was missing. When I moved to the United States to work for Microsoft, I decided to gift myself a digital piano for my birthday. It wasn't a grand investment—literally—but it was a symbolic step back into the world of music.

I found a supportive and welcoming community through piano meetups in the Redmond area. These were people like me—professionals with full-time jobs who were also deeply passionate about music. Their encouragement reignited my soul, and this time, I approached the piano with a new mindset. I chose the pieces I wanted to play, set my own goals, and even began participating in local competitions. My ultimate dream? To one day compete in the prestigious Cliburn Amateur Piano Competition.

For me, coding and piano are deeply connected. When I'm coding and hit a roadblock, I take a break and play the piano. The act of creating music clears my mind and helps me see coding problems from new angles. It's almost magical how solutions seem to reveal themselves when I return to work after a session at the piano. This practice not only enhances my productivity but also keeps my passion for both coding and music alive.

Balancing these two demanding pursuits requires meticulous time management. I structure my day carefully, carving out time for practice, work, and personal life. I've learned to view my piano practice not as an extra task but as a way to unwind and recharge.

But staying on fire without burning out requires more than just good scheduling. I've learned the importance of setting realistic goals and listening to my body and mind. I'll never forget a time in Canada when I pushed myself too hard preparing for a music exam. I fell in love with a complex piece that was far beyond my skill level and ignored my teacher's advice to start with something simpler. The result? I injured myself, hated the piece I once adored, and couldn't touch the piano for months. That experience taught me a valuable lesson: ambition is important, but so is understanding your limits and pacing yourself.

At work, I'm strategic about managing my workload. I communicate openly with my manager about my priorities and current commitments. When new tasks come my way, I make sure we discuss what can be deprioritized, so I don't feel overwhelmed. This open dialogue helps me stay productive and prevents burnout.

I appreciate and am lucky to have a strong support system. My boyfriend encourages my passions, whether it's meeting a tight work deadline or practicing piano for hours. My manager at Microsoft has been instrumental in supporting my interests outside of work. Knowing that I have this network of understanding and encouragement gives me the confidence to pursue my goals in both coding and music.

That said, I'm careful to separate work from my personal life. During business meetings, I keep the focus strictly on work unless someone asks about my piano hobby. If they do, I'm happy to share—but I respect the boundaries between these two worlds.

Maturity has brought me a new perspective on goals and dreams. I'm no longer rigid about where I want to go in my career or my music. I've learned to embrace the surprises along the way. For instance, I now find performing on stage more nerve-wracking as an adult than I did as a child. But instead of letting it discourage me, I take it as a challenge, handling it one small step at a time.

Whether it's exploring new coding projects, participating in chamber music, or one day competing in the Cliburn, I stay open to where these passions will take me.

Staying on Fire Without Burning Out

The key to balancing my passions and career is simple but powerful:

- **Know your limits:** Recognize when you're pushing yourself too hard and take breaks to recharge.
- **Set achievable goals:** Focus on a few meaningful objectives rather than overwhelming yourself with too many.
- **Communicate openly:** Be honest about your commitments with your manager and loved ones.
- **Build a supportive network:** Surround yourself with people who encourage and uplift you.

These principles have allowed me to stay on fire without burning out, fueling both my career and my love for piano. Life isn't about choosing between your passions and responsibilities—it's about finding harmony between them. And when you do, the results can be nothing short of magical.

■ ■ ■

Imagine a cat, err, better yet, a Shewolf tiptoeing along the edge of a skyscraper, focused and graceful, every muscle in sync. She's poised, determined, and unshaken by the dizzying height. That's us when we're on fire—navigating the precarious balance of ambition and responsibility. But staying on that ledge too long, without rest, can lead to a fall.

As women, we often find ourselves navigating the delicate balance between pursuing our dreams and carrying the weight of expectations and even criticism—both those placed on us by others and the ones we quietly place on ourselves.

"You're too old to play basketball again."

"You want to go to a conference in the United States with a small child at home?"

"You've never written a book—are you sure you can do it?"

I've heard these questions, these doubts, so many times. Maybe you have, too. The fears and skepticism of others often reflect their limitations, not yours. The path to making things happen requires us to shake off the doubts of others and tune into what drives us. Whether you're daring to dream big or taking one small step toward a goal, the fire has to come from within—and it has to be sustainable. Amelia Earhart once said, "The most difficult thing is the decision to act; the rest is merely tenacity." She was right. Dreaming is the first step. But after that, success lies in discipline, grit, and time management.

For me, "making it happen" has meant:

- Unlocking Modern Work Cloud adoption in Poland's finance sector, by integrating legal and technological frameworks, and out-of-the-box thinking.
- Fighting to finish my Erasmus program in Lisbon when my boyfriend, now husband, and I had just 2 euros a day to live on.
- Finding a basketball team in every city I've lived in—whether Lisbon or Józefów, a small Polish town—because the court was my sanctuary.
- Organizing three editions of the EmPower Women Program despite budget constraints and limited support.
- Writing this book while working full-time, with no prior experience, and trusting my instincts to partner with Miri.

None of these accomplishments came without its challenges, but each one was fueled by passion, joy, and a clear sense of purpose.

And perhaps just as importantly, they were achieved without burning out. From my experiences and the incredible stories of the women in this chapter, I've distilled a few lessons that have helped me—and others—stay on fire while preserving our well-being. Achieving your dreams is rarely a smooth journey—it takes perseverance and grit to push through setbacks and stay the course over time. Grit isn't about quick bursts of effort; it's about keeping your fire burning steadily, even when the path gets challenging. Discipline plays a big role here, but it doesn't mean striving for perfection. Instead, it's about consistency—breaking your goals into manageable pieces, building routines, and sticking to them. Progress, no matter how small, adds up. Along the way, it's vital to find what truly fills your cup. What energizes and sustains you? Is it time with friends, exercise, or moments of solitude? Passion alone isn't enough; you need to regularly replenish your energy by leaning into the people, activities, and spaces that restore you. Most importantly, listen to your body and mind. As you have seen, burnout doesn't arrive with a loud announcement—it sneaks in through subtle signs like fatigue, irritability, or a fading sense of joy. Pay attention to these cues because if you're not well—mentally, physically, or emotionally—your fire can't burn brightly. Staying inspired and balanced isn't just about working hard; it's about caring for yourself along the way.

So here's my advice: Dream big. Stay on fire. But don't forget to step back when the flame gets too hot. Rest when you need to. Trust yourself enough to know that you're capable—and that you don't have to do it all at once.

If you find yourself chasing your dreams and feel the weight of expectations pulling you down, think of this: The fire that drives you is powerful, but it's not limitless. Tend to it carefully. Feed it with joy and purpose, not perfectionism and overwork.

Chapter Recap

- Burnout creeps in when we ignore our limits. Pay attention to early signs like fatigue, irritability, and diminished joy.

- True success comes from sustainable effort and adaptability, not chaos of chasing everything.

- Allow yourself to change and grow over the years. Fuel new areas of interest and don't feel guilty for shifting your focus to what matters most at different stages of your life.

Embracing the Journey

Burnout isn't a sign of failure—it's your body and mind's way of telling you it's time to prioritize yourself. Self-care is not an indulgence; it's essential. Take regular breaks, practice mindfulness, nurture your connections with loved ones, pursue hobbies that bring you joy, and always establish healthy boundaries to protect your well-being.

Chapter 9
Learn-HER-Alls

Carry yourself with confidence, back yourself with competence
—author unknown

At the beginning of this book, we explored the idea that confidence isn't just about what we achieve or the feedback we get from others—it's about something much deeper. It's shaped by our beliefs about our own capabilities, those stories we tell ourselves about what we're good at, what we can do, and who we are. Those beliefs aren't just a backdrop to our lives. They actively shape how we experience the world, how we learn, and how we grow. Confidence is built over time, yes—but it's also deeply tied to what we believe about ourselves and the world around us.

Here's where it gets fascinating—and a little unnerving. Our preconceptions, those ingrained ideas about what we're capable of and how the world works, don't just sit idly in the background. They actually play a starring role in how we process new information and how we grow. In the book *How People Learn: Brain, Mind, Experience, and School* by Bransford, Brown, and Cocking, the authors break it down beautifully.

> ### Impact on Learning
>
> **Misconceptions:** If your preconceptions are off-base—if they're wrong or rooted in fear—they can steer you into misunderstandings or reinforce patterns that don't serve you.
>
> **Constructive Learning:** But here's the good news: if you're willing to dig into those preconceptions, examine them, and even challenge them, they can become a foundation for deeper, more meaningful learning.
>
> **Engagement:** When we acknowledge and address those beliefs, we create bridges. New information connects to what we already know (or think we know), and that connection makes learning stick.

In summary, the beliefs you hold about yourself—your origin story, your identity, your strengths and weaknesses—are constantly shaping how you learn and grow. Sometimes, these beliefs act like a powerful lens, sharpening your focus and guiding your growth. Other times, they're more like a brick wall, keeping you stuck, unable to move forward.

Let me say this a little louder for the people in the back: Your preconceptions can either be your stepping-stones or the very chains that hold you back. And here's the scariest part—those very beliefs might convince you that there's nothing more to learn, that you've got it all figured out. "Oh, I've been doing this forever—I've nailed it." Or, "This has always worked for me; why would I change now?" Sound familiar? It does to me, because that mindset once defined a part of the culture at Microsoft.

Being a "know-it-all" is not just a smug attitude. It creates an environment where preconceptions aren't just walls; they're fortresses. That attitude, the "I already know everything worth knowing" mentality, had its consequences. It bred a competitive, high-stakes culture where being the smartest person in the room wasn't just valued—it was expected. We calibrated our work, our worth, and even our energy levels to match this perfectionist, cutthroat standard. And in the process? Burnout thrived. It was like we were trying to outsmart each other into exhaustion.

So, which came first—the ruthless, burn-yourself-out competition, or the know-it-all attitude that fueled it? Which is the chicken, and which is the egg? Honestly, it doesn't really matter. The point is, the cycle fed itself, and it wasn't sustainable. I remember coming in fresh from the outside, full of ideas, eager to learn and share my perspective. But I quickly realized nobody wanted either of those things from me. Learning? Sharing? Forget about it. If you had knowledge, the unspoken rule was to keep it locked up tight. Because if someone else "learned from you," they might take that knowledge, use it to their advantage, and win the game. Collaboration and innovation? They were barely existent on the field.

This culture wasn't universal—it varied across different parts of the company and around the world. When I talked to Izzy about it, she had a different perspective. She joined Microsoft in 2011 as the sole woman on the Premier Field Engineer team, a group of highly skilled technical specialists. Unlike my experience, she received exceptional support from her colleagues—not because she was a woman, but because she was a professional joining a crew of "super-skilled ninjas," each of whom had mastered every feature of the product. These engineers believed in a support system, openly sharing their knowledge with her and backing her up on tough customer cases. To Izzy, the "know-it-all" culture wasn't about hoarding knowledge—it was Microsoft's approach to rigorous product development in the server world. But what was universal is how the culture began to shift collectively for the positive. As Microsoft started listening more attentively to customers, the focus moved from knowing everything to learning constantly. The company became curious, customer-obsessed, always striving to improve.

This cultural shift from "knowers" to "learners" coincided with Microsoft's transition from servers to the cloud. It wasn't just a digital transformation; it was a mindset transformation that helped us thrive. Shedding the skin of a tech dinosaur wasn't easy, but it was essential. And here's what we discovered: that being a "learn-it-all" was less about acquiring new knowledge and more about unlearning. It was about finding the courage to let go of old stories, habits, and assumptions that no longer served us, making space for something better.

Becoming a learn-it-all encompasses the emotional work of clearing out outdated beliefs and tired narratives, opening yourself up to new ideas, fresh lessons, and deeper understanding. Unlearning isn't for the faint of heart—it's messy, uncomfortable, and often takes more courage than learning itself. It requires the humility to say, "Maybe I was wrong," or, "Maybe there's a better way." When we unlearn, we make room for curiosity to breathe, to expand, and to lead us toward transformation.

And here's where it gets exciting: that new education, that fresh perspective? It's a ticket to independence and, you guessed it—confidence. Real, grounded confidence. Not the kind that's propped up by perfectionism or fear, but the kind that comes from knowing you're not stuck, from trusting yourself to adapt and grow. Such is the journey of Purna Virji, Principal Content Solutions at LinkedIn, and what she discovered when she embraced the learn-it-all mentality at Microsoft.

Linked and Learning

I grew up in India with my brother, and if there's one thing deeply ingrained in many of us from a young age, it's that education is the key to success. It's not just a saying;

it's practically a mantra. Ask anyone from India, and they'll nod knowingly. Education is drilled into us as the ultimate path to self-sufficiency, stability, and dignity.

But for girls like me growing up in India, there was an added layer. In many families, including mine, it was understood that boys inherited everything—the family wealth, property, legacy. Girls? Well, we were expected to marry, settle into domestic life, and depend on our husbands. For many girls, that was the script: be a good wife, manage the household, and leave financial independence to the men.

I knew early on that wasn't the life I wanted. I wasn't a rule-follower or docile by any stretch of the imagination—I was a rebel. I wanted to carve out my own path, to be self-sufficient and empowered. I didn't want to rely on anyone else to shape my future. I realized that for me, education was more than just a societal expectation; it was a ticket to independence, to freedom, to living life on my terms.

Education as Empowerment

That deep, intrinsic understanding of education as empowerment stayed with me as I pursued a degree in journalism at Cardiff University in the UK and eventually moved to the United States. My first job was an internship in television, but this was the early 2000s, and digital marketing was just beginning to explode. I could see the world shifting, and I made a deliberate choice to lean into this new frontier.

I didn't just dip my toes in—I dove in headfirst. I sought out mentors, read blogs, and relentlessly taught myself the ins and outs of digital marketing. Back then, it was all about self-driven learning because there weren't formal courses or structured paths for this emerging field. I was intentional about asking my company to invest in my growth by sending me to workshops, particularly for advanced Google Ads training.

I realized something crucial during that time: if I wanted to be the best in my field, I had to make learning a priority. I worked late into the nights and spent my weekends upskilling myself. I wasn't afraid to be stubborn about my education because I knew it was the best investment I could make in myself.

I also looked to people like Avinash Kaushik and John Gagnon as inspirations—leaders in the space who were pushing boundaries. But I noticed something glaringly absent from the stages they spoke on: there were no Indian women, no women of color at all. That realization lit a fire in me. I decided not only did I want to excel in this field, but I also wanted to open doors for others like me.

Becoming a Teacher to Learn

As I soaked up knowledge from blogs, conferences, and mentors, I started giving back by teaching others. This wasn't just an altruistic move—it was a way to solidify my own learning. You know the saying: To teach is to learn twice. Every time I shared what I knew—whether through publications, conference talks, or workshops—it deepened my understanding.

And there was a practical bonus: being a speaker at conferences meant I didn't have to pay to attend, giving me access to even more knowledge from other experts. The cycle of learning, teaching, and growing became a cornerstone of my career.

A New Opportunity at Microsoft

Eventually, this passion for education and advocacy led me to Microsoft. I got introduced to the role at one of the very conferences where I had been speaking. The position was on a brand-new team with a dual focus: part evangelist, part learning and development (L&D). The goal was to educate customers about the possibilities and opportunities within Microsoft Advertising, and I couldn't have been more excited.

It was like Disneyland for me. I got to travel the world, work with customers, and learn on the job. Every session I prepared for and every conversation I had with marketers—whether they were from small businesses or global giants like Amazon—taught me something new. I delved into the mechanics of how sales teams operated, how pricing strategies were developed, and how support differed across different customer segments.

With my past decade of working both in-house and agency-side, I was able to connect with customers on a peer-to-peer level. I could step into their shoes as a marketer and help them with practical, actionable insights. The work was fulfilling, and the program's success snowballed. Soon, other regions were inviting me and my colleagues to share our expertise globally.

Traveling the world, meeting new people, and educating others while being paid to do what I loved—it was a dream come true.

The LinkedIn Challenge

After five incredible years at Microsoft, a friend introduced me to an opportunity at LinkedIn: a role as a content marketing evangelist. I took the leap, but it was a steep learning curve. Three months in, I felt like I was starting over at a brand-new company.

It was the middle of the pandemic, full lockdown mode. I had never met my team or my stakeholders in person. The budget was tight, and the expectations were sky-high. My job was to convince hundreds of thousands of LinkedIn advertisers to see the value in our platform and invest more in LinkedIn Advertising.

I was overwhelmed. But instead of spiraling, I took a deep breath and went back to the foundation that had always guided me: education.

Education as the Answer

I asked myself, could education be the key to scaling this challenge? I remembered everything I had learned about customer education from my time at Microsoft and started building a case for it. I gathered statistics, studies, and examples to show my leadership how investing in education could drive adoption of our products and help our customers succeed.

We started small, focusing on one segment of customers in North America. The results were astonishing: customers in this pilot group sometimes spent 40–45% more than others in their segment.

The program quickly gained traction, spreading across markets and time zones. I eventually led a global team of 12 people, transforming what began as a bubbling idea into a full-fledged customer education program. This initiative didn't just boost product adoption; it empowered our customers to find real success with their investments. And for me, that mutual success—lifting others while achieving business goals—is what education is all about.

■ ■ ■

Purna's perspective and benefits on embracing the learn-it-all mindset speaks to my heart. For me, this *unlearning* journey has been less about becoming something new and more about returning to something that's always been within me: that fresh, curious, and open mindset I had before my ego crept in—before it convinced me to play it safe, to act like I had all the answers, and to avoid vulnerability.

Embracing a growth mindset requires letting go of ego's grip, releasing the need for certainty and control, and welcoming back our truest selves. That part of us—the wide-eyed, curious, and fearless part—is still there. It's the part that isn't afraid to ask questions, to stumble and try again, to approach the world with excitement and possibility. When we allow that self to take center stage, our personal stories become richer, braver, and far more meaningful than we ever imagined.

Just look at Stacy Tatem, former Solution Specialist at Microsoft, as she embraced her return to her most authentic self.

Cloudy with a Chance of Learning

Looking back on my career, one principle has guided me: the power of being a learn-it-all. My journey to Microsoft wasn't linear—it began at Morgan Stanley and transitioned into tech sales, where I discovered a career that fueled my passion for growth and learning. Without a college degree initially, I worked hard to gain experience, eventually saving enough to enroll in Boston University's degree completion program. This determination, paired with my success building high-performing sales teams, helped me land a role at Microsoft in 2008, covering major accounts for Dynamics.

Joining Microsoft was thrilling but daunting. As a single mom to a spirited toddler, navigating tech sales was no small feat. My exceptional boss, Beth, was instrumental in my success. She championed mentorship and holistic support, teaching me to balance work and life without guilt. Her emphasis on self-care, setting boundaries, and continuous learning reshaped my approach to both my career and motherhood.

The tech landscape in 2008 was rapidly evolving. Azure and cloud computing were just beginning to take center stage, and with Beth's mentorship, I learned to stay ahead by embracing curiosity and adaptability. The lessons I absorbed—resilience, innovation, and the value of collaboration—helped me thrive at Microsoft and inspired me to pay those lessons forward.

In 2013, I left Microsoft to explore new opportunities, but my journey with the company wasn't over. In 2019, I returned as a Partner Manager for Microsoft Learn, where I blended my passion for sales with upskilling. This role allowed me to lead projects that empowered professionals to thrive in an ever-changing digital world. Witnessing individuals transform their lives through learning reaffirmed the importance of embracing growth at every stage of life.

This passion extended to my involvement with Women in Cloud, where I advised women entrepreneurs on scaling their businesses and becoming Microsoft Partners. One project particularly close to my heart was helping a Georgia-based entrepreneur develop a program to teach Microsoft technologies and combat generational poverty. These experiences underscored the transformative impact of education and mentorship, especially for underrepresented communities.

My advocacy for upskilling expanded into the cybersecurity space. Serving as a judge for Women in Cybersecurity and attending global events like the Cybersecurity Women of the World conference inspired me to deepen my understanding of this critical field. Today, I am pursuing a Master of Science in Criminal Justice with a focus on Cybercrime at Boston University, driven by a desire to address the growing threats in our digital world.

Every step of my journey—from tech sales to upskilling projects and now cybersecurity—has reinforced the benefits of being a learn-it-all. Microsoft gave me the platform to grow, learn, and contribute meaningfully to a dynamic, evolving industry. Along the way, I've seen firsthand how embracing challenges, seeking mentors, and staying curious can change lives—including my own.

■ ■ ■

Indeed, as women, it's not only essential to seek out new learning opportunities and mentors willing to teach and guide us, but also to identify a platform where we can continue to grow and build as we learn. Just as in tech development, there's a "stack"—a collection of technologies working together to create a functional system. Whether it's a software stack, technology stack, or data stack, understanding the individual components and how they integrate is critical for success in modern applications. In much the same way, an ever-evolving learn-it-all mindset lays the foundation for continual growth, allowing us to build upon our experiences and knowledge in layers. It's a process Dr. Renate Strazdina, D.Sc., National Technology Officer Central Europe at Microsoft, aptly calls "knowledge stacking."

My Journey of Continuous Learning

In school, I was an average student—solidly in the upper quartile but far from extraordinary. My true learning journey began at 18 when I started studying computer science. It was then I discovered my passion for bridging technology with real-world challenges. A question has guided me ever since: "What does this mean in the real world?" This curiosity fuels my drive to explore new theories, products, and processes.

Over the years, my intrinsic motivation has led me to dive into fields like accounting, banking, healthcare, bioengineering, cybersecurity, and sustainability. To see how technology can enhance these areas, I've needed to understand them. The rapid pace of innovation keeps my learning list ever-growing, and I find immense fulfillment in the process. Continuous learning isn't just a necessity—it's a source of joy that deepens my understanding and allows me to share knowledge in meaningful ways.

Knowledge Stacking

When tackling a new subject, I start with the basics. Even in areas where I have formal education, like artificial intelligence or cybersecurity, I revisit foundational principles before diving deeper. For example, with the rise of Generative AI, I reviewed core AI concepts first to better grasp its applications. Real-world examples help me connect theory to practice, making it easier to share insights and visualize how technology can solve practical problems.

I embrace "knowledge stacking," a concept popularized by David Epstein in *Range: Why Generalists Triumph in a Specialized World*. By layering knowledge across diverse fields, I've discovered how combining technical expertise with soft skills—like storytelling, public speaking, and team management—unlocks creativity and innovation. I may not aim to master every domain, but I learn enough to collaborate effectively and identify how technology can better serve specific industries.

Connecting the dots between technology and real-world needs brings me immense satisfaction.

You might wonder, "How do you find the time?" I understand the challenge of balancing work, family, and learning. During my doctoral studies, I worked full-time in consulting, and while completing my ACCA certification I was caring for my young daughter. I even postponed my final exam for six months because I was too exhausted. Through these moments, I learned the importance of prioritization and embracing imperfection.

When motivation wanes, I take one small step—reading an article, watching a video, or tackling a single task—to maintain momentum. I also create a yearly learning plan, which provides structure and direction.

I've realized that the hardest moments—when new material feels overwhelming—are where the most growth happens. Pushing through this discomfort leads to deeper understanding and lasting knowledge.

Sharing knowledge is one of the most rewarding aspects of my journey. Whether it's explaining complex concepts to colleagues or helping students connect the dots, these moments reinforce my belief in the power of continuous learning to foster collaboration and innovation.

By working with university students, I share what I've learned, just as my professors once did for me. It's one small way I can contribute to making the world a better place.

Continuous learning is vital—not just for personal growth, but for adapting to a constantly changing world. Every new skill and perspective opens doors to opportunities, fuels creativity, and contributes to well-being. Learning is a lifelong adventure, and I'm committed to exploring, growing, and sharing as I move forward.

■ ■ ■

At Microsoft, continuous learning isn't just a slogan—it's a core part of who the company is today. This shift goes beyond mindset, with tangible investments in reskilling, upskilling, and new skilling initiatives that span the globe. Through programs like the Global Hackathon and employee-driven initiatives, Microsoft is creating spaces where learning, innovation, and empowerment thrive. Susie Kandzor, Senior Director of Hacking in The Garage at Microsoft, tells us how.

Empowering Every Person

The Hackathon is not just an event, it's a pivotal movement that underscores our dedication to democratizing innovation. It's about empowering every individual, irrespective of their role or level, to share their ideas and work on projects they're truly passionate about. This represents a significant cultural shift for us—transitioning from a "know-it-all" to a "learn-it-all" mindset—a principle that has been fundamental to our strategy for fostering innovation. When diverse, cross-functional teams come together, they bring unique perspectives and skills to the table, creating an environment where real breakthroughs can occur. None of this would be possible without the steadfast support of our leadership, including CEO Satya Nadella, who ensures we have the resources and encouragement to turn these ideas into reality.

The Global Hackathon, the world's largest private hackathon, is a shining example of Microsoft's growth mindset. Every September, more than 70,000 employees from every division and region of the company come together online and in person to bring their ideas to life. Open to employees of all skill levels and roles, the Hackathon fosters creativity and collaboration, resulting in groundbreaking projects like the Xbox Adaptive Controller and sustainability-focused initiatives like FarmBeats.

If you're looking to bring the energy and impact of a hackathon to your company, start small. The principles of democratizing innovation can work at any scale—whether you're working with a single team or an entire organization. Encourage employees at all levels to contribute their ideas and feel empowered to make a difference. It's about fostering a culture of innovation where everyone feels included.

Creating an environment where people know their ideas are truly welcomed and valued is one of the most powerful things a leader can do. Building a learn-it-all culture, where curiosity and growth take center stage, doesn't happen overnight. It requires time, intentionality, and a willingness to navigate challenges along the way. But here's the truth: the effort is absolutely worth it. The results—greater innovation, deeper engagement, and a community of empowered individuals—are nothing short of transformative.

■ ■ ■

Microsoft's growth mindset culture inspires us to create grassroots programs that address specific and nuanced needs. These initiatives are driven by individuals in the field who take the lead in both their development and execution. Here are some of these impactful programs—fueled by a passion for growth and inclusion—that are transforming lives and creating new opportunities for women worldwide.

- **emPower Women (Poland):** A program that equips women in customer organizations with the confidence and skills to bridge IT and business, empowering them to lead digital transformations.
- **Girls Nail IT (Czech Republic):** A mentorship initiative inspiring young girls to explore careers in technology through real-world experiences and hands-on learning.
- **TechHer (UK):** A platform supporting women's professional and technical growth through workshops, networking, and career development initiatives.
- **Women Rising (Australia):** A leadership program that has helped more than 9,000 women globally—employees, customers, and partners—build confidence, refine skills, and step into leadership roles.

Michelle Markham, ANZ K-12 Education Director, tells us more about the Women Rising program.

When Women Rise

About six years ago, we realized that despite our efforts, we weren't attracting, retaining, or promoting enough women into leadership roles in the Australian subsidiary at Microsoft. We needed a more impactful solution, so we explored various options and came across the Women Rising program. Women Rising is an eight-module program spread over four months, designed to unlock the potential of women and help them advance in their careers. Each module focuses on different aspects of personal and professional growth. The first module encourages women to reflect on their life and career goals, helping them define their vision and purpose. The second module addresses Imposter Syndrome and inner critics, empowering women to lean into their strengths. The remaining modules cover essential leadership skills, including communication, conflict management, navigating workplace politics, executive presence, and well-being. The program also teaches women how to find and use mentors and sponsors effectively. It's managed by an external company, and the decision to participate in an external rather than developing our own was driven by several factors:

- **Rich Content and Expertise:** The Women Rising program provided rich, data-driven content that would have been challenging and time-consuming for us to develop internally. The program's structure and materials were already well established and proven effective. Participants go through the program with women from various companies worldwide, creating a supportive community.

- **Focus on Implementation:** By outsourcing the program, we could focus on implementation and support rather than content creation. The program includes videos, personal play sheets, live coaching calls, and an online forum for discussions. It would be a really immense amount of work to develop on our own, on top of our daily duties. This allowed us to dedicate our resources and energy into facilitating the program and ensuring its success within our organization.

- **Scalability and Reach:** The external program enabled us to scale quickly and reach a broader audience. Since its inception, more than 9,000 women globally, including more than 1,000 from Microsoft, have completed the program. We could include women from various regions and even extend the program to our customers and partners, creating a larger impact.

This program has been highly successful in Australia, empowering women with practical leadership tools and unlocking their potential. Its success stems from three key factors: its deeply personal approach, the built-in accountability of women progressing together, and the shared language it fosters within organizations—such as the widespread use of a brand survey at Microsoft Australia. Additionally, its four-month duration strikes the right balance, allowing for meaningful commitment and self-reflection. As an alumna of the Women Rising program myself, I can personally attest to its impact. It helped me build confidence and advance from an individual contributor to a manager, and eventually to a manager of managers. Beyond individual growth, the program has also transformed workplace culture, increasing female leadership and strengthening support networks.

■ ■ ■

As technology evolves, staying ahead requires a commitment to lifelong learning. The World Economic Forum[1] underscores the importance of skills like AI and digital literacy in shaping the workforce of the future. Programs like Microsoft's Skills for the Future[2] are addressing this need by partnering with governments and organizations to deliver cutting-edge AI training at scale.

For women in tech, this moment is pivotal. Industry leaders are making it clear: upskilling in AI is no longer optional—it's essential. AI and emerging technologies are transforming the world at an unprecedented pace, and the ability to grow and adapt is the key to staying relevant and thriving in this new era. This is our time to step forward. Don't stay on the sidelines—embrace this wave of transformation as a creator, a builder, and a leader. Dive into areas like prompt engineering, explore the vast AI ecosystem, and claim your place in shaping the future. The opportunity to grow, lead, and innovate is here—and it's yours to seize. So, don't wait for permission. Take charge of your learning journey today. The future is calling, and you are ready to answer.

You can start immersing yourself in the Era of AI by taking free courses available online. Microsoft offers a few, including: Introduction to Generative AI,[3] Azure AI Fundamentals,[4] Develop Natural Language Processing Solutions with Azure AI Services,[5] Streamlining Your Work with Bing Chat,[6] and Embrace Responsible AI.[7]

A learn-it-all is someone who embraces that spirit of curiosity—the desire to learn everything there is to possibly learn. To leave nothing unexplored. Think back to the girl you once were—the one who saw the world with curiosity. The one who marveled at how the letters of the alphabet could spell out your name. That girl is still within you, and now it's her time to etch her name into the new world of AI.

I speak from a place of personal conviction because I, too, have stepped into this space—not as a coder, but as a creator and a visionary. The theme of this book has been code and confidence, and while I may not write the code myself, I have built the confidence to ideate something bold and meaningful. This is how Empressa.ai was born—a platform designed to empower women to navigate and thrive in the AI age. Empressa is not just a tool; it's a movement. It's a space where women can come together, learn from one another, and embrace AI with confidence and curiosity. The goal is simple: to ensure that women are not just participants in this revolution but leaders of it.

AI is no longer a concept of the future—it's here, transforming the world around us. As it evolves, so must we. In Chapter 12, we'll dive into the near future to explore upcoming innovations and the possibilities they hold. But for now, let's focus on preparing ourselves for what's ahead. Let's reconnect with the curious, determined girl within us and step confidently into this new era—ready to learn, ready to create, and ready to leave a lasting legacy for the women who will follow in our footsteps.

Chapter Recap

- A learn-HER-all is a woman who's traded in the need to be a know-it-all for the courage to be a learn-it-all—open to learning, unlearning, and growing every step of the way.

- Don't wait for permission. You don't need it. This is *your* learning journey—own it, start today.

- Continuous learning isn't just about picking up new skills. It's about building the kind of independence, resilience, and confidence that helps you rise strong, no matter what life throws your way.

Embracing the Journey

Teaching is learning twice. Learn how AI can assist with your hobbies or interests, master a specific AI tool, and then inspire your friend. Watch both of you deepen your wisdom and confidence together.

Chapter 10

Fitting Room—Leadership Comes in All Shapes and Sizes

Adornment is never anything except a reflection of the heart.
—Coco Chanel

When I first envisioned this book, my excitement stemmed from a clear vision: to bring together women leaders from across Microsoft and around the world to share their journeys. What inspired me most was how much we can all learn by reflecting on the experiences and lessons that shape us. Storytelling carries a unique power—it connects us, inspires us, and celebrates our journeys. I wanted to create a space to capture that power and highlight the stories of incredible women who are redefining leadership in their own voices, on their own terms at Microsoft and beyond.

Curious, I asked Copilot how many books exist on leadership. While it couldn't provide an exact number, it suggested there are likely more than 15,000 in print today. That's staggering. You've likely read at least a few—or maybe even an entire shelf. But this chapter isn't another checklist of "seven leadership principles" or "ten traits of great leaders." Instead, it's deeply personal: a reflection on what I've observed and learned through this project, and from the extraordinary women who graciously shared their stories. Together, they've shown me what it means to lead authentically, purposefully, and in a way that's uniquely their own.

I decided to call this chapter "The Fitting Room," not just as a nod to the metaphorical "rooms of the house" we've explored throughout this book, but because the fitting room is a place of discovery, experimentation, and reflection. It's where we try on new outfits, make adjustments, and seek honest feedback from those we trust. It's a space where curiosity and courage meet. In much the same way, these women approach leadership as a process of intentionally choosing and layering qualities that reflect their values, experiences, and unique leadership styles. Their qualities of leadership feel like a carefully curated wardrobe—each piece thoughtfully selected, purposeful, and reflective of the impact they aim to make.

Impactful leadership today is much like curating a wardrobe—an intentional and exciting process that many of us can relate to. After all, who doesn't love a little shopping? Just as we carefully select what we wear to reflect our identity, leaders choose the qualities and values they embody each day to inspire trust, foster connection, and create environments where people thrive.

In today's world, great leaders don't just focus on outcomes—they build relationships through key traits like empathy, humility, and patience. Interestingly, these so-called soft skills are often considered feminine traits,[1] which means that women naturally bring a leadership style rooted in human connection, not trends. Now, I invite you to step into the Fitting Room with me, where we'll explore how these women have chosen their signature pieces—carefully curating a wardrobe that reflects the unique strengths, values, and leadership styles that define who they are.

Vasu's Couture

Out of the corner of my eye, I catch Vasu Jakkal, CVP Security, poised and radiant, a beautiful sight of strength and grace. When I first met Vasu, I was struck by how effortlessly she wears her values. Vasu's journey is a masterclass in leading with a steadfast commitment to impact. As a trailblazer in engineering, leadership, and cybersecurity, Vasu represents the She in her highest form.

When reflecting on her career, Vasu shared a powerful truth: too often, as women, we close doors on ourselves. We look at opportunities and tell ourselves, "I'm not the right fit," or, "I don't have the right background." But that's simply not true. This conviction drives her passion for inclusion and inspires those around her to challenge their own self-imposed limitations. In cybersecurity, where women make up just 25% of the workforce, fostering a sense of belonging is both a challenge and a priority. For Vasu, leadership means encouraging women to take on new opportunities, even when they feel intimidating. She encourages women to step into the fitting room, try on bold new pieces, and embrace their full potential with confidence and purpose.

Tailored for Purpose

Stepping into the fitting room of leadership, Vasu's wardrobe is built on a foundation of intention. At the heart of her style is her "P-Framework"—a collection of five essential values that she wears with purpose. These guiding principles form the timeless staples of her leadership wardrobe, ensuring she is dressed for every challenge and opportunity.

Purpose

Purpose is the tailored top that holds Vasu's entire wardrobe together, grounding her in every decision she makes. Rooted in her family's history of service—her grandparents were part of India's freedom movement—her purpose is about impact, not accolades. "Purpose matters deeply and comes before all else," she says. Every action she takes aligns with her values, ensuring she leads with a mission-driven mindset.

Passion

If purpose is the foundation, passion is the bold statement piece that makes her leadership style unforgettable. Vasu's energy is contagious, igniting enthusiasm in everyone she works with. "Passion isn't just what drives me—it's what I instill in the people I work with," she says. Like a vibrant accessory that lights up any outfit, her passion adds energy to everything she touches.

Possibilities

Possibilities are Vasu's signature sunglasses—the visionary lens through which she views the world. A natural "possibility thinker," she sees challenges not as obstacles but as opportunities waiting to be unlocked. "Every setback is a doorway to innovation," she explains. Her perspective inspires her teams to push boundaries and embrace creative problem-solving, ensuring they're always looking forward with optimism and ingenuity.

Positivity

Positivity is the lightweight but durable coat that Vasu throws on when the weather gets tough. Optimism is her superpower, shielding her from negativity and helping her lead her teams through difficult times with grace. "A positive perspective can transform even the toughest situations," she says.

People

At the center of Vasu's wardrobe is her people-first mindset—a comfortable and timeless piece she wears every day. For Vasu, leadership is about uplifting others, ensuring everyone feels valued, and creating an inclusive environment where all voices are heard. "Leadership is about connection," she says. "It's about building deep relationships and empowering others to succeed."

Vasu's journey hasn't been without challenges. She began her career in 1999 as an engineer at Intel, designing semiconductor chips in a male-dominated field. Like many women, she initially felt the pressure to suppress her natural style in order to fit in. But a transformative moment came when she held her newborn daughter for the first time. It was then that Vasu decided to lead with her own style. "I realized that being my whole, authentic self was the key to happiness," she shares. From that moment, she redefined leadership on her own terms—bringing optimism, gratitude, and openness to every space she entered.

One of Vasu's most remarkable qualities is what she calls "compassionate strength." Rejecting the outdated notion that kindness is a weakness, she shows that empathy amplifies authority rather than undermines it. "Kindness and strength go hand in hand," she explains, proving that a compassionate leader can inspire trust, loyalty, and collaboration.

Her work in cybersecurity exemplifies this balance of strength and compassion. In a field where 7,000 password attacks happen every second, Vasu remains calm, hopeful, and forward-thinking. She approaches her work with optimism and a collaborative spirit, likening her leadership style to King Arthur's Round Table: inclusive, empowering, and focused on collective success. This approach not only drives innovation but also aligns with Microsoft's mission to create a safer, more inclusive digital world.

As a woman in cybersecurity, Vasu is deeply committed to increasing diversity and fostering a sense of belonging. "Our superpowers lie in showing up as our true selves," she says. Her goal is to encourage women to step into this space with confidence, knowing their unique perspectives are needed now more than ever. She also emphasizes the importance of women being allies to one another. "We rise by lifting others," she says, championing collaboration over competition.

Catwalk Essentials

When Vasu steps onto the runway, she models a style of leadership that is timeless and transformative, inspiring others not to imitate her but to design their own unique collections.

Her wardrobe is stitched together with the influence of her role models. At its core is the strength, compassion, and positivity of her mother, who remains her greatest inspiration. Vasu also draws from the wisdom of Mahatma Gandhi, whose commitment to nonviolence taught her the power of leading with humanity, and from Satya Nadella, whose transformative leadership at Microsoft demonstrates that innovation thrives best when paired with empathy. These influences serve as the fabric of her leadership, but it's Vasu's unique flair that makes it shine.

Every day, she steps onto the runway with purpose and optimism. Her mantra is clear: "There's no act of brilliance or kindness too small to matter. Life is too short not to bring your best self and your superpowers to the table every single day."

As Vasu walks down the runway, she models leadership lessons that serve as the signature pieces of her collection. Each one is bold and practical, inspiring others to design their own ensembles for success.

1. **Self-awareness:** Vasu begins her leadership look with the most essential layer: self-awareness. "Knowing what brings you joy and aligns with your strengths is the foundation of effective leadership," she explains.

2. **Confronting Imposter Syndrome:** Beneath every outfit is an inner lining of courage—a layer that bolsters Vasu's confidence and helps her manage the Imposter Syndrome that so many leaders face. "You are your own worst critic," she reminds us. Rather than letting self-doubt unravel her, Vasu confronts it head-on, engaging in an open dialogue with her fears and moving forward boldly.

3. **Sponsors and Mentors**: Vasu's leadership wardrobe wouldn't be complete without the guidance of trusted tailors—her sponsors and mentors. "The people who challenge you, believe in you, and push you to grow are invaluable," she says.

4. **Taking Risks:** Vasu knows that no great collection is without a bold statement piece. Inspired by Brené Brown, she embraces risk as an essential part of leadership. "Dare greatly," she urges. "It's not about avoiding failure—it's about how you rise after falling."

Vasu's wardrobe reminds us that true leadership isn't about fitting into a mold—it's about breaking it. Her collection reflects her individuality while inspiring others to embrace their own unique styles.

Monalisa Smile

When Monalisa Sengupta, Partner Director of PM for Copilot Agents and the Teams Ecosystem at Microsoft, enters the fitting room, she brings a distinct and purposeful approach: she leads with full confidence in her team, and a deep commitment to purpose. Her journey showcases what's possible when strength is paired with empathy, and innovation is guided by integrity. Monalisa's journey from an individual contributor with no technical background to a senior leader in engineering has been shaped by lessons in self-discovery, collaboration, and the supportive culture of the Microsoft platform, which values and rewards diverse backgrounds.

Reflecting on her early career, Monalisa shares, "I didn't think of it as leadership at the time, but I naturally brought people together to achieve results. I confidently shared my thoughts, even among colleagues with 20 or 30 years of experience. Thankfully, those early mentors and managers recognized my potential and encouraged me to see leadership as my strength." That recognition became the foundation for a leadership style built on trust, empowerment, and clarity.

As she transitioned into her first managerial role, Monalisa began asking herself the deeper questions: "What kind of leader do I want to be? What truly matters to me?" Over the years, she developed a leadership philosophy rooted in her values. Her approach prioritizes listening, trust, and enabling others to excel—qualities that define her ensemble.

Tailored for Purpose

Trust as a Foundation

Monalisa leads with an unshakable belief in the potential of others. "I always assume that everyone wants to do a good job," she says. "My role is to identify their strengths, provide structure, and guide their energy effectively."

This trust extends to her mantra: "Drive for my people to be better than me." She intentionally builds teams with skills that surpass her own, creating environments where talent thrives. "My leadership approach is to create the right structure, bring intelligent people together, and set clear outcomes. From there, I trust my team to deliver—and they do."

Ensuring Every Voice Is Heard

One of Monalisa's core wardrobe pieces is making sure everyone has a voice. "Even if I disagree with someone's perspective, I want them to share it," she says.

However, she also believes in explaining her reasoning transparently when decisions need to be made. "I respect everyone's perspective, but if I have clarity on the direction, I ensure my team understands the 'why' behind my decisions."

Connecting the Dots

Monalisa has an exceptional ability to synthesize complex information, identify patterns, and bring clarity to her team. She likens this skill to orchestrating music: "It's like there are 25 audios playing at once, and my job is to create the right harmony from them." For years, she assumed this was something everyone could do, until a manager helped her realize it was one of her greatest strengths.

This skill enables her to provide her team with clear guidance and direction, empowering them to perform at their best. "Every individual wants to do their best. My job is to give them the environment, structure, and clarity to make that possible."

Leading Beyond Labels

Monalisa's philosophy of "Let's talk work" has defined how she navigates the challenges of being a woman in a male-dominated industry. "Biases existed before I was born and will exist after I die," she says. "But I don't carry the weight of those biases with me. When I step into a room, I focus on what's right for the business and the customer."

She doesn't frame herself through the lens of her gender. "I've never walked into a room thinking of myself as a woman leader.

I've always walked in as someone ready to deliver." Her approach is pragmatic: she addresses conflicts or misunderstandings with data-driven clarity, always prioritizing what's best for the customer and the organization. "If people have a problem with my gender, that's their problem—not mine. I'm here to do the work."

Catwalk Essentials

Monalisa's style of leadership encompasses a piece for every stage of the runway:

1. **Know Yourself.** Monalisa believes self-awareness is the cornerstone of effective leadership. "It's essential to understand what matters to you and how your priorities change over time. Reflect on those shifts, and decide how much you're willing to compromise and how much you want to preserve." For her, knowing yourself also means embracing your strengths and being honest about your weaknesses. "You don't need validation from others to know your worth. Be confident in who you are, lead decisively, and make choices that align with your values."

2. **Embrace Self-validation.** Monalisa openly acknowledges the challenge of seeking external validation in leadership roles. "Validation feels good, but relying on it can hinder your progress," she says. Over the years, she's worked on embracing self-validation, learning to trust her instincts rather than seeking approval from others. She shares a personal anecdote: "When I started weight training, my trainer often criticized my posture or form. But I showed up every day, determined to improve. One day, she praised my persistence, and it felt incredible. That

moment reminded me how tempting it is to rely on external praise, but real growth comes from within."

3. **Show Up.** Monalisa believes showing up is half the battle in leadership. "Even when you're unsure or don't feel like it, showing up for your team is non-negotiable. By being present, you set an example of resilience and commitment. The rest will follow."

4. **Communicate with Clarity.** For Monalisa, effective communication is about simplicity, brevity, and empathy. "You need to understand your audience and tailor your message accordingly," she advises. She's a firm believer in the mantra: "Be crisp, be clear, be gone." Time is precious, and leaders must make their points efficiently while ensuring clarity and alignment.

Monalisa finds inspiration in everyone she meets, believing that every person has something valuable to teach. One of her most significant role models is Arianna Huffington, who turned her collapse from exhaustion into a mission to promote wellness and challenge toxic work cultures. "Her advocacy for emotional health in the workplace has been a powerful example of how leaders can use their influence for meaningful change."

Monalisa's ability to laugh at life's absurdities is a hallmark of her grounded leadership. She recounts a humorous incident where a CIO assumed she was an assistant to a junior feature Program Manager. "When the account team corrected him, his face went white, and he awkwardly apologized. I laughed it off and said, 'Let's move on.' Life is too short to take everything personally. Sometimes, you just have to laugh and keep going." We hear that!

"Leadership is about creating environments where others can thrive. It's not about ego—it's about impact," she says.

Sarah's Staples

As Sarah Mocke, Vice President, Engineering & Architecture, joins us inside the fitting room, her presence radiates a bold confidence—a fusion of technical mastery and collaborative spirit. With more than two decades at Microsoft, her journey is less about following a predefined style and more about crafting her very unique one. Her walk is deliberate, showcasing pieces that represent persistence, innovation, and a love for the craft.

Sarah's leadership style isn't just about technical brilliance; it's about the layers she's intentionally added over the years—trust, collaboration, and a commitment to fostering creativity. As she strides forward, her collection tells the story of a leader who embraces growth, values the voices around her, and consistently leads with heart and purpose.

Tailored for Purpose

Staying True to Your Craft

At the heart of Sarah's style is her enduring love for technology—a timeless trench coat she wears with pride. "There's this idea that career growth has to follow a linear path to be meaningful," she says. "But my journey has been anything but conventional." While some may focus on climbing the ladder quickly, Sarah has stayed connected to the craft she loves, coding and pursuing a master's degree in cybersecurity even as a vice president.

"Some might see my growth as slower, but to me, it's been immensely rewarding because I've stayed connected to what I love."

Cultivating Collaboration

Sarah's style is defined by collaboration. Her "non-conflict culture" fosters an environment where passionate conversations are encouraged, but the focus remains on solving problems, not personal disagreements. "Dynamic, passionate conversations are essential," she says, "but it's always about the work, never personal."

Her approach—running her team like an academic peer review—ensures ideas are critiqued constructively, not emotionally. The result? A culture where creativity flourishes and trust thrives. "We critique to elevate the work, not tear down the person," she explains.

Trust and Recognition

Sarah wears trust and recognition like a bold statement necklace—something that draws attention and reminds her team of their value. She invests deeply in understanding her team members' motivations, aligning their roles with their passions, and celebrating their achievements.

One of her signature initiatives, a technical awards program, gives team members visibility into leadership meetings, opening doors to growth. "It's about creating opportunities for my team to shine," she emphasizes.

Calm Under Pressure

Navigating high-pressure situations is one of Sarah's greatest strengths, and she does it with the poise of walking in resilient heels—steady and unshakable. Whether managing customer crises or guiding her team through unforeseen challenges, she focuses on breaking down complexity and enabling decisive action. "I've developed a calmness in tough situations," she reflects. "It's about taking one step forward and helping others do the same."

Authenticity and Adaptability

At the core of Sarah's wardrobe is her authenticity, worn like a beloved denim jacket—practical, approachable, and versatile. "Leadership isn't about perfection—it's about persistence, passion, and staying true to who you are," she says.

As the role of technical leaders evolves, Sarah adapts without losing sight of her values. "It's no longer about being the best at a single programming language—it's about understanding secure coding practices, collaborating effectively, and embracing new technologies," she shares.

Catwalk Essentials

As Sarah takes her place on the leadership runway, her style is as much about practicality as it is about inspiration. Here are her key pieces of advice for leaders curating their own wardrobes for the catwalk:

1. **Start with Self-Awareness.** Self-awareness is Sarah's compass, guiding her decisions and keeping her aligned with her values. "Knowing what brings you joy and aligns with your strengths is the foundation of effective leadership," she says. This accessory ensures that no matter where the journey takes her, she remains grounded and intentional.
2. **Manage Imposter Syndrome.** Even seasoned leaders like Sarah face moments of self-doubt. Meeting global leaders can trigger Imposter Syndrome, but she counters it with an invisible layer of confidence: "I tell myself, 'You're here for a

reason. You belong at this table.'" This layer is her secret weapon, allowing her to lead with courage even in moments of uncertainty.

3. **Surround Yourself with Mentors.** Just as every great outfit needs fine tailoring, every leader needs mentors and sponsors to help refine their craft. "The people who challenge you, believe in you, and push you to grow are invaluable," Sarah says. Her toolkit includes a network of trusted advisors who help her sharpen her leadership style.

4. **Take Risks.** For Sarah, leadership means daring greatly. Inspired by Brené Brown, she sees failure as an essential part of growth. "It's not about avoiding failure—it's about how you rise after falling." Whether it's experimenting with a new approach or tackling a challenging project, Sarah's bold accessories remind us that risks are necessary for innovation.

On the leadership runway, Sarah's style is a powerful reminder that the best leaders aren't afraid to blend their technical brilliance with humanity. By staying true to her passions, valuing the voices around her, and embracing growth with open arms, she shows us how to walk the runway of leadership with confidence, impact, and authenticity.

Carissa on the Runway

Carissa Rouse, Director at Microsoft, enters the fitting room with a quiet confidence that commands attention—not for its flashiness, but for its charisma. With a leadership style intricately tied to her career at Microsoft, Carissa represents the essence of a modern leader—one who challenges norms, uplifts others, and redefines success on her own terms.

Her journey, much like a well-curated runway show, has been anything but conventional. From her beginnings as a vendor, navigating personal and professional challenges, to becoming a respected leader of high-performing teams, Carissa has built her leadership wardrobe with care and intention. Each piece she wears tells a story of resilience, self-discovery, and the courage to lead with integrity and purpose.

Tailored for Purpose

Authenticity

Carissa's leadership style begins with authenticity—a signature piece she wears with confidence and care. "To find your most authentic self, you also have to find out who you are not," she reflects. Authenticity, for her, is about bringing her true self to the table while knowing how to share wisely. "Not everyone deserves a front-row seat to your life," she says, emphasizing the importance of discernment.

Her authenticity is what makes her relatable and inspires trust. Whether it's her love of Taylor Swift GIFs or her ability to infuse humor into high-pressure situations, Carissa creates an environment where others feel empowered to bring their full selves to work.

Resilience

Resilience is Carissa's weatherproof coat, built to withstand storms and adapt to changing circumstances. From growing up in financial hardship to becoming a mother of three at a young age, her life has been shaped by challenges that she chose to face head-on. "There were days I felt less than those around me," she admits. "But those experiences taught me resilience and showed me the value of staying true to myself." Carissa views resilience as an "energy" she brings to her teams. By demonstrating this resilience, she inspires her teams to "match her energy," helping them perform effectively under pressure.

Compassion and Inclusion

Carissa's compassion and commitment to inclusion are the warm, wraparound scarf she wears with pride. One of her greatest strengths is fostering collaboration and building diverse teams. This ability has been praised by long-tenured employees and has inspired others to seek opportunities to work under her leadership, whether as team members or direct reports.

Carissa rejects traditional hiring molds, focusing instead on potential and personality dynamics—a forward-thinking approach that later became known as Microsoft's "screen in" method.

Side note: Did you know that she was on the interview panel to hire Miri Rodriguez into a new, internal role? This is where they met, and became soul sisters ever since!

"The social skills I developed to survive became the skills I could use to thrive," she explains. Whether mentoring women in tech, bridging gaps between technical and non-technical teams, or challenging exclusionary dynamics like the "boys' club" and the "mean girl's club," Carissa's style symbolizes her dedication to creating a workplace where everyone feels valued and included.

Emotional Intelligence

Carissa's emotional intelligence is like a pair of elegant earrings—subtle yet impactful, bringing clarity and focus to her leadership style. She prioritizes what truly matters, advising others to "focus on what deserves your time and attention." This ability to filter out trivial concerns allows her to maintain balance and make thoughtful decisions, even under pressure.

One of her most innovative moves was seeking a millennial mentor to stay relatable and relevant, a decision she credits as pivotal in her growth.

Innovation and Creativity

Carissa's knack for making technical concepts accessible, or "speaking geek," is her statement belt—a functional yet bold accessory that pulls everything together. Her innovative mindset drives her to think beyond conventional boundaries, whether it's creating technical awards programs to spotlight her team's achievements or mentoring across generations.

"Hard work doesn't have to mean miserable work," she says, reminding us that innovation flourishes in environments where people feel inspired and engaged.

Catwalk Essentials

As Carissa struts her fabulous self down the runway, she offers invaluable lessons for those curating their own styles:

1. **Authenticity Is Your Foundation.** "To lead authentically, you must first know who you are," Carissa advises. Authenticity isn't about full transparency—it's about balancing vulnerability with professionalism and sharing wisely. This foundation ensures that every piece you add to your leadership wardrobe reflects your true self.
2. **Resilience Is Built Through Adversity.** Carissa's story is a testament to the power of resilience. "Many of us break barriers in bite-sized chunks," she says. Leadership isn't about grand gestures—it's about showing up every day, even when it's hard, and striving to be just 1% better.

3. **Inclusion Is Key to Innovation.** Carissa's commitment to inclusion has shaped her teams and her leadership style. She believes in hiring for potential and creating environments where diverse perspectives thrive. "The best teams are built on trust, collaboration, and respect," she says. Inclusion isn't just an accessory—it's central to creating lasting impact.

4. **Emotional Intelligence Drives Balance.** Carissa emphasizes the importance of prioritizing what matters most. By focusing her energy on meaningful goals and decisions, she has maintained clarity and balance throughout her career.

5. **Creativity Sparks Connection.** Whether it's her ability to "speak geek" or her initiatives to recognize and celebrate her teams, Carissa's creativity sets her apart as a leader. To her, creativity isn't just about ideas—it's about connecting people and making work both impactful and enjoyable.

And there you have it—a full New York Fashion Week *a la tech* celebrating the She leadership traits the Microsoft women wear so well. Each one shines in her own style, walking her own path, and making an impact in her own way. Their garments are as unique and stunning as they are, the styles are diverse, the colors bold, and the silhouettes varied, yet certain staples remain timeless—authenticity, empathy, curiosity, and strength. These women wear them effortlessly, like second skin. They are the same qualities we recognize across the boardroom table, in a shared glance of mutual understanding, or even in the briefest encounter on the Metro.

"Nice shoes."

"Lovely jewelry piece."

We exchange smiles, silently appreciating the beauty of these invisible adornments that radiate confidence, capability, and grace. They're more than just traits; they are the invisible threads that weave together the fabric of what it means to lead with intention. These garments not only signal leadership but also invite and inspire others to step into their own power and potential.

But once in a while, I catch sight of a She whose outfit appears a little worn. Her shoes may be scuffed, her confidence dulled by the weight of time or circumstance. Her brilliance hasn't faded—it never does—but perhaps she's forgotten how to let it shine, or maybe she's waiting for someone to remind her of her worth.

"It's time for a promotion," I think to myself. "Does she know this? More importantly, is she going to ask?"

In the next chapter, we'll step into the complex and often untidy world of job promotions. We'll hear the stories of women who refused to settle, who navigated the obstacles in their paths, and who fought unapologetically for their rightful seats at the table. Together, we'll explore the strategies, the setbacks, and the victories that define the journey of claiming not just a role, but the power, recognition, and opportunities every woman deserves.

Chapter Recap

- Certain qualities—like confidence, capability, and grace—are universal hallmarks of great leadership. These traits inspire and empower others to step into their own potential.

- Even the best leaders may experience moments of self-doubt or feel undervalued. During these times, a reminder of their unique strengths and worth can reignite their confidence.

- Leadership is not one-size-fits-all. It comes in many forms, and there is space for everyone to lead authentically, embracing their own unique style.

> **Embracing the Journey**
>
> How boring would it be if we all looked and dressed the same? Take the time to find and embrace the uniqueness in your leadership—and fashion—style. Both are powerful expressions of who you are inside and out. Because in leadership, as in fashion, the best looks are the ones you create for yourself.

Chapter 11

Get That Promotion

The only tired I was, was tired of giving in.

—Rosa Parks

Wow. That last chapter was powerful. Reading it, I felt something shift—like I could lace up confidence the way I'd pull on my favorite boots and finally ask for what I deserve. The moon. That long-overdue promotion I've been waiting on since before COVID-19.

Because let's be honest—those years were chaos. People lost lives. And jobs. Companies restructured. And me? I told myself I was just grateful to still be here. But this year? No more waiting. I've done the work. I've put in the late nights. I've juggled the never-ending demands of work, family, friendships, workouts, and the invisible labor that comes with just being a woman in the world.

That's right. I'm stepping into my power and walking straight into the life I want.

Tomorrow.

Or maybe the day after.

I just don't know where to start.

Sound familiar? Yeah, too damn familiar. As women, we lace up our confidence like Taylor Swift slipping into those 7-inch Louboutins—ready to own that well-deserved promotion. We've put in the work. We've earned every bit of it.

And then—*bam!*—we slam right into that old, familiar wall. The odds? Definitely *not* in our favor.

A study from MIT Sloan found that women are 14% less likely to be promoted than their male colleagues, despite often receiving higher performance ratings. And research from LeanIn.Org and McKinsey & Co. shows that for every 100 men promoted to a managerial role, only 87 women make it to the same level.

I'm not sharing this to discourage us—it's not about despair. It's about breaking the cycle so many of us get caught in: the belief that "if I just work hard enough, I'll get the promotion," or "if I keep my head down and do everything right, someone will notice." Let's call that out for what it is. That mindset hasn't worked, and it won't work. As the saying goes, insanity is doing the same thing over and over again and expecting different results.

In today's workplace, it's time to change how we show up—just like we've changed how we work with new tools and technologies. It's not just an opportunity; it's our responsibility to stand up, speak up, and advocate for the recognition and advancement we deserve.

Here's the good news: we're not in this alone. I've gathered stories from women who've done exactly that—women who've navigated the messy truths, learned hard-earned lessons, and proven that it's possible to move up. They've got the good, the bad, and everything in between to share. So, let's dive right in!

Rita Robbins, AI and Executive Speaking Coach: A Masterclass in Courage and Connection

Picture this: Microsoft had just welcomed Satya Nadella as its new CEO. The excitement was palpable as employees across the company tuned in to hear his inaugural vision for the future. Rita, like everyone else, sat in eager anticipation, ready to hear what their new leader had to say.

But as Nadella began to speak, something became clear—his passion was outpacing his delivery. His excitement propelled him forward, and his words tumbled out quickly, leaving many in the audience struggling to follow. The closed captions couldn't keep up, and neither could Rita.

Let's pause here. Most of us, in that moment, would feel the frustration bubbling up. Maybe we'd lean over to a colleague to vent quietly or resign ourselves to feeling disconnected. Someone else will address it, we'd think. But not Rita.

Rita recognized something important in that moment: it wasn't just about her struggle to follow along. It was about the thousands of employees, from all corners of the globe, who were grappling with the same challenge. She saw the bigger picture—this was about connection. And in that moment, Rita made a decision rooted in wholehearted leadership.

She sent Nadella a message. Yes, Satya Nadella, the newly minted CEO of Microsoft. Just think about the courage that took. She wasn't sure how her message would be received—or if it would be received at all. But she sent it anyway.

Her note was direct and honest. She explained how, as a native English speaker, she'd struggled with his pace and accent during the speech, noting that the closed captions couldn't keep up either. But her message didn't stop at the problem. Rita also advocated for the audience, writing: "We all want to know what you're saying, and we're all excited to hear your vision. This is important for us as employees, and we want to share in your enthusiasm for the future."

And then something extraordinary happened. Ten minutes later, her ping lit up. It was Nadella himself. He didn't just thank her—he apologized. He acknowledged her feedback and asked a question that cracked the door wide open: "Do you have any suggestions?"

What followed was a conversation that would leave a lasting mark on both of them. Rita shared her expertise as a Master Trainer, offering practical tips: pause after commas and periods to give the audience time to process; slow the pace to ensure clarity; and be mindful of the 60% of Microsoft employees who weren't native English speakers and relied on closed captions.

When the call ended, Rita thought, *That was nice. But what now?* She braced herself for potential blowback—after all, she had just critiqued the CEO. But she also stood firm in the knowledge that she had done the right thing, not just for herself but for everyone eager to connect with their new leader.

A month later, Nadella took the stage again at the next corporate meeting. This time, something was different. His speech was slower, more deliberate. He paused after punctuation. The closed captions flowed seamlessly, capturing every word. The audience followed. The vision landed.

Ten minutes after the meeting, Rita's ping lit up again. "How was that?" Nadella asked.

"Great," Rita responded. "Clear, paced, and CC caught it beautifully. Thank you so much!"

But it didn't stop there. By the third meeting, Nadella had taken it to another level. His pace was impeccable, his articulation sharp. Rita didn't even need the captions. When Nadella followed up again, he shared something remarkable: he'd been working with a linguistics coach. He had taken her feedback to heart and turned it into action.

And that's the beauty of this story. It's not just about Satya's humility or Rita's courage—it's about the power of speaking up when it matters. Rita didn't just improve her own experience; she improved communication across an entire organization.

Her boldness set off a ripple effect. Employees connected more deeply with their leader. Ideas flowed more freely. And years later, her act of courage opened doors she hadn't even imagined. Microsoft's

Marketing organization approached her to become an Executive Speaker Coach, helping leaders craft authentic, impactful messaging about AI. Why Rita? Because she had become synonymous with impactful communication grounded in empathy and clarity.

If you're sitting here wondering how to ask for that promotion, how to make your voice heard in a crowded room, or how to step into your power as a leader, let's take a moment to reflect on Rita's story.

The traits that made her journey possible—courage, vulnerability, authenticity, and the willingness to take bold steps—are qualities that already exist in each of us. They're the traits we often bury under doubt, fear, or the belief that someone else will step forward first. But Rita's story is proof of what happens when you lead with your whole heart.

Here are the takeaways we can carry forward:

- **Be Bold:** Don't wait for someone else to fix the problem. Your boldness could be the catalyst for change.

- **Advocate for Others:** Speak up—not just for yourself, but for the broader community. Connection thrives on honesty.

- **Own Your Expertise:** Don't underestimate the value of what you bring to the table. Offer insights that only you can provide.

- **Be Willing to Grow:** Feedback isn't just a gift for others. It's an opportunity to grow together, as Rita and Satya both demonstrated.

- **Leave a Legacy:** Leadership isn't just about what you achieve; it's about the impact you leave behind.

■ ■ ■

Rita's story is a great reminder that when we show up, speak out, and lead with authenticity, the ripple effects can reach far beyond what we imagine. But let me be honest with you—it's not as simple as just knowing you have the traits of courage and authenticity. I wish it were. We all wish it were. Because even when you embody those qualities and bring your full self to the table, the systems we operate in often aren't set up to reward you. Rita made it look effortless. But the truth is that she was working against all the odds that are still stacked against us today. And the data doesn't lie. Here are more sobering stats:

Representation in Managerial Positions: Globally, women hold just 28.2% of managerial roles.[1] While that represents progress, it also means that two-thirds of these positions are still held by men. Leadership parity remains an aspiration, not a reality.

Leadership Roles: Out of the Fortune 500, only 10% of CEOs are women.[2] Women hold 28% of board seats globally,[3] which is a step forward, but nowhere near where it should be. The message? Breaking into top leadership positions remains an uphill battle.

Economic Impact: Here's a statistic that stops you in your tracks: If we closed the gender gaps in employment and entrepreneurship, global GDP could increase by 20%, according to the World Bank.[4] This isn't just about fairness. It's about unleashing economic, social, and global potential that benefits everyone.

Workplace Discrimination: More than half of women report experiencing gender discrimination at work.[5] That's not just a number; it's a lived reality for millions of women. And we know how deeply this discrimination impacts opportunities for advancement.

Now let's pause here, not to dwell on the frustration but to acknowledge both the progress and the pain points these stats represent. Yes, we've come a long way. But the road to true gender parity in leadership remains steep, uneven, and fraught with barriers. So, what do we do with this knowledge? What do *you* do with this knowledge? Because if you're here, reading this, I know you're not the kind of person who's content to sit on the sidelines.

What I've learned from my own journey into vulnerability and courage is that while the systems we operate in might not be designed for us, they don't get to define us. They don't get to dictate whether we show up, whether we take up space, or whether we ask for what we deserve. Yes, the statistics remind us of the reality we're operating in. But they also remind us why it matters so much that we continue to show up, to speak up, and to step forward.

When you think about asking for that promotion, raising your hand for that high-stakes project, or speaking your truth in a room full of power and privilege, you might hear that nagging voice whisper: What if they say no? Or worse: What if I'm not good enough?

Let me tell you something I know for sure: the cost of staying silent, of not stepping up, is far greater than the cost of hearing "no."

Because every time you choose to step into the arena—every time you dare to risk failure or rejection—you're not just advocating for yourself. You're creating space for others to follow. You're showing them what's possible. Every courageous act chips away at those statistics, reshaping the narrative for the women who come after us. Rita didn't wait for permission to speak up. She didn't wait for the perfect moment or a guaranteed outcome. She saw a need, and she filled it. She dared to challenge the CEO of one of the most influential companies in the world, not because it was easy, but because it was necessary. And her boldness didn't just improve communication across Microsoft; it reshaped the trajectory of her career. It set her on a path where her courage and advocacy opened doors she hadn't even imagined.

The stats may be stacked against us, but they aren't immovable. And every time we choose courage over comfort—every time we raise our hand, ask for what we need to advocate for ourselves—we're proving that those numbers don't tell the whole story.

Marisela Cerda, Director Azure Business Program Management: A Lesson in Boldness and Self-Advocacy

Take Marisela Cerda. In July 2017, she sat in front of her laptop, tears streaming down her face, rereading an email she had written—a letter she poured her heart into but never sent. After 16 years at Microsoft, the email represented something far greater than a collection of words. It was a declaration of her self-worth, a refusal to continue being underpaid, unrecognized, and underappreciated.

With fall promotions just a month away, Marisela had made a firm decision: this would be the last time she allowed herself to be overlooked for a Director-level position—known at Microsoft as Principal.

But here's the twist: she never sent that email.

When September came, so did the news—Marisela finally received her promotion. She had scaled the steep, rocky hill of corporate America. Not by waiting for recognition, but by deciding she deserved it and boldly pursuing it. Yet those tears she cried while writing that unsent email weren't just about the climb—they were about the hard-earned lessons she learned along the way. Lessons she hopes others, particularly women and underrepresented groups, won't have to learn the hard way.

Marisela's experience sheds light on this truth: navigating the path to leadership is rarely straightforward, especially for those whose journeys weren't part of the blueprint. As a Latina and a first-generation corporate employee, Marisela didn't have a road map. The corporate ladder wasn't built with her in mind.

She quickly learned that for many women and minorities, the climb isn't just about skill or performance—it demands self-advocacy, resilience, and the ability to strategically create opportunities where none exist.

Her journey wasn't a straight line, nor was it easy. Early in her career, after years in a senior position, Marisela broached the topic of promotion with her manager. The response was a disheartening mix of doubt and dismissal: "Getting high rewards at Principal is cut-throat. It may not be something you want to move to."

The words, while likely intended to protect her, landed with a sting that Marisela couldn't shake. For months, she wrestled with the idea that maybe she wasn't capable of stepping into that role. But deep down, she knew this wasn't about her abilities—it was about the limitations others had placed on her.

And so, she made a bold decision: she needed a manager who believed in her potential and would support her ambitions.

When Marisela moved to a new role with a manager who shared her vision, she laid her cards on the table from day one. "I want to be a Principal, and I'll need your help to get there."

It was a simple statement, but a powerful one. In saying the words out loud, Marisela created alignment between her ambitions and her team's support.

She worked tirelessly, excelling not just in her role but also expanding her scope of influence. She began building relationships with Directors and Principals, seeking their feedback and learning from their experiences. But even as she sought insights, she noticed something disheartening: there were few, if any, role models who shared her background.

The few White women she consulted with admitted that their promotions had been a surprise—they hadn't asked for them; they had "just happened." Marisela realized that for her, the "just happened" route wasn't an option. She would have to make it happen.

Marisela understood a critical truth: promotions aren't just about being good at your job. They're about showing leadership, creating impact, and taking ownership of opportunities.

With clarity and intention, she began strategizing her next steps. She identified areas where she could make the biggest difference and worked tirelessly to deliver results that exceeded expectations. But she didn't stop there. She also focused on visibility—ensuring that her contributions were known, understood, and valued by decision-makers.

She learned to advocate for herself, to speak up in rooms where her voice might otherwise have gone unheard, and to unapologetically own her aspirations. By the time the fall promotions were announced, Marisela had transformed not just her career, but her approach to it.

When I think about Marisela's story, what stands out most isn't just her tenacity or her success—it's the lessons she learned along the way and the way she embodies them for others.

Marisela's tears that July weren't just about frustration. They were about the resolve to refuse to settle for less than she deserved. And her story is a reminder that the climb to leadership isn't about waiting for permission or hoping to be seen. It's about showing up, speaking your truth, and refusing to let the system tell you what you're capable of.

Her journey offers lessons for all of us, particularly women and those from underrepresented groups:

State Your Intentions: Don't assume others know what you want or where you're headed. Be bold in naming your ambitions.

Find Allies: A supportive manager or mentor can make all the difference. Seek out people who will advocate for you and challenge you to grow.

Build Relationships: Promotions aren't just about what you do—they're about who sees your work and how they perceive your potential. Build a network of allies and champions.

Own Your Growth: The path to leadership requires more than skill. It requires intentionality, visibility, and a willingness to ask for what you need.

■ ■ ■

Marisela's story is a great example of what happens when you decide you deserve more—and you go after it with clarity, courage, and resilience. She claimed her space with rigor and got what she deserved. And then there's Imane's story—a fierce reminder of why taking risks matters, especially when that corporate ladder doesn't come with clear rungs. From being one of the few women in her industrial engineering class to earning Microsoft's prestigious Pinnacle Award, her journey is proof of what's possible when boldness and determination collide.

Imane El Majdoubi, Enterprise Commercial Lead UAE: A Journey of Bold Moves and Big Wins

Imane began her career in Morocco, working for a multinational consulting firm, followed by a tech regional system integrator. By 2011, however, she was ready for something bigger. When a public sector account executive role at Microsoft was recommended to her, the hiring manager initially refused to interview her, doubting her ability to navigate relationships with government officials.

She was only 26, but Imane had already decided one thing: she would not let someone else's doubts define her.

When the manager finally agreed to meet her, he wasn't subtle about his skepticism. "Who do you know personally at this customer?" he asked dismissively, implying she lacked the connections to succeed. When she responded with names, he sarcastically clarified, "I meant people you work with personally, not you heard of."

Instead of being rattled, Imane reached for her phone and offered to dial the senior executives she had worked with. Calmly, confidently, she let her work and relationships do the talking. That moment—when her quiet confidence shifted the entire dynamic of the interview—set the tone for her career at Microsoft. It wasn't about proving she belonged; it was about demonstrating it.

Imane's career has been defined by bold moves and calculated risks. After 8 successful years in Microsoft Morocco earning multiple awards, Imane reached a crossroads and her careers options at home were limited. She could stay in her comfort zone or take the leap into the unknown by relocating to Dubai for a new regional role managing global system integrators and advisory firms in the Middle East and Africa.

The decision wasn't easy. Uprooting her daughters and leaving behind her family, friends, and support system was daunting, but Imane knew that growth doesn't happen in comfort zones. "Taking risks is essential for growth," she reflects. Imane had a good job with prospects for a new role in 2 years, but she aimed higher and believed in her potential for greater achievements. "You can't climb the corporate ladder from your comfort zone."

Her move to Dubai marked a turning point. She expanded her network, built connections across, built connections across the region, and gained visibility both internally at Microsoft and externally in the market. Her unconventional work with the global system integrator across MEA opened the door for a bigger role leading the financial services industry in UAE. Imane believes that: "The best way to plan for your next promotion is to deliver an exceptional impact in your current role." She delivered impressive results, including quadrupling key business areas over 3 years, developing a strong team and attracting great talents a key accomplishment that showcased her people leadership skills and ability to drive strong business impact.

Imane emphasizes that while delivering results in your current role is critical, so is being intentional about your career. "Nobody is going to knock on your door with a promotion," she says. "You have to plan for it, create opportunities, and make your aspirations known." This makes it easier for leaders who recognize talent and are open to hiring based on potential to notice you. Imane's hard work didn't go unnoticed. Her exceptional results earned her Microsoft's Pinnacle Award—an honor reserved for those who exemplify leadership and deliver significant impact. A year later Imane was promoted to a leadership role in the UAE managing the Enterprise business across all industries.

But Imane is quick to acknowledge that success comes with sacrifices. "There is always a cost," she says. "For me, moving meant leaving behind my support system and missing precious moments with my daughters as we adjusted to a new environment. But I've always believed that when I'm fulfilled professionally, I'm a better mother." I remember the tough preparation for the 2019 NY marathon, leaving my running group back home and training alone in Dubai's 40 degrees heat. But, crossing the finish line felt more fulfilling than any previous run.

Here are the lessons Imane's journey teaches us:

- **Let Actions Speak Louder Than Words:** Imane's calm confidence during her interview—demonstrating her connections rather than defending them—set the tone for her leadership style.
- **Be Intentional About Your Career:** Delivering results is vital, but so is making your aspirations clear. Plan your career with purpose, and don't be afraid to articulate your goals.

Build Relationships: Success isn't just about what you know; it's also about who knows you and understands your impact.

Balance Comes in Different Forms: Sacrifices are part of the journey, but fulfillment in one area of life can make you stronger in another.

The She stories on getting that promotion share a powerful common thread: the courage to take control of their own narratives. The She doesn't wait for permission or expect someone else to clear the path for her success. Instead, she embraces boldness, seeks support from allies, and creates opportunities where none exist.

■ ■ ■

And finally, we hope Harpreet's story inspires you to put yourself first—even when others might label it as "selfish" or "self-centered." Because when you embrace boldness, adaptability, and self-advocacy, you're not just climbing the ladder—you're flipping the whole damn thing and redefining what success looks like on your own terms.

Hapreet Kapour, Principal Technical Program Manager: Redefining Leadership

When Harpreet joined Microsoft, she was stepping into one of the most transformative times of her life—pregnant with her second child and entering the high-stakes world of one of the largest tech companies on the planet. As a brown woman in tech, a Sikh woman wearing a turban, and a former management consultant from India, her transition was as daunting as it was exhilarating.

She often found herself as the only woman—and the only woman of color—in rooms filled with male engineers. And it didn't take long for the reality of those dynamics to surface. Harpreet vividly recalls her first leadership meeting, which her manager had invited her to attend as a "learning opportunity." Sitting in the conference room, surrounded by polished shoes and sharp suits, she felt small. Her cultural upbringing, where women were often encouraged to "keep their heads down and not ruffle feathers," echoed in the back of her mind.

But what happened in that meeting changed everything. She watched as one of her colleagues presented an idea she had shared privately over coffee—without crediting her. It was a defining moment. "I made a vow that day," Harpreet reflects. "I wouldn't just sit at the table one day—I'd own it."

Harpreet quickly realized that success wasn't just about working hard; it was about learning the unspoken rules of influence and visibility. She began building credibility with her manager and colleagues, ensuring her voice was heard by presenting her own ideas. Within weeks, she shifted from being a quiet observer to a bold contributor.

Her path to her first promotion, however, wasn't straightforward. "Getting that first promotion felt like climbing an ice wall without crampons," Harpreet shared. Pregnant and preparing for maternity leave, she decided to take a bold risk that turned heads—she approached her manager with a promotion plan.

"Even discussing a promotion while pregnant made people think I was crazy," she admitted. But Harpreet was clear about her potential, her goals, and the impact she could make. Determined to prove her value, she volunteered to lead a high-stakes, high-visibility project that everyone else had avoided. The project's complexity and visibility didn't deter her; instead, she saw it as an opportunity to build cross-departmental relationships and deliver measurable results.

By the time the next review cycle came around, Harpreet didn't wait for recognition. She presented her case for promotion with data, testimonials, and tangible outcomes. "This time, there was no 'let's see,'" she said proudly. "I got the title and the raise."

But Harpreet's journey wasn't without challenges. Her boldness, while effective, wasn't always welcomed. "Some colleagues—mostly men—labeled me as 'too ambitious' or 'intense,'" she shared. A senior director even told her she needed to "soften her approach" if she wanted to succeed.

At first, she questioned herself, wondering if she was being too assertive. But as she looked around at her male counterparts, whose assertiveness was celebrated, not criticized, she had a revelation: This isn't about me; it's about the expectations placed on women like me.

"That's when I made another risky decision: I wouldn't compromise my authenticity to fit into a mold that wasn't designed for women like me," she affirms.

Harpreet sought out mentors—women who had faced similar struggles—and leaned into their wisdom. One mentor gave her a piece of advice that became her guiding principle: "Own your narrative. Don't let anyone else write it for you." (Sound familiar? Smile.)

Owning her narrative became more than just excelling at her job. It meant advocating for herself and others, championing underrepresented voices, and driving initiatives that created opportunities for others to shine. "By lifting others, I built a coalition of allies who supported my leadership," she explained.

Over the years, Harpreet continued to take bold, unconventional steps in her career. Most recently, she made a calculated move to share her vision for a leadership role within her organization—a step many would deem risky. She presented her strategies for the role, aligning them with the company's goals, her unique experience, and her own development plan.

"The odds may not be in my favor, but I've made my case," she said, once again demonstrating her characteristic courage and strategic mindset.

Harpreet is honest about the costs of her bold moves. "There were sacrifices—missed family dinners, sleepless nights, and moments of profound self-doubt," she shared. She lost friendships with colleagues who couldn't reconcile her success with their own insecurities. And there were battles she fought and lost, each one leaving scars that taught her resilience.

"But the gains far outweigh the costs," she said. Harpreet has become a role model for women in her organization and industry, proving that it's possible to lead without losing yourself. She has learned to navigate office politics without compromising her integrity and has redefined what success looks like—not just for herself, but for the women who will come after her.

Harpreet's story offers a powerful blueprint for women seeking to rise in their careers:

- **Take the Risk:** Don't wait for the perfect opportunity. The riskiest paths often lead to the most rewarding destinations.
- **Advocate for Yourself:** Speak up for your achievements and your worth—because no one else will do it for you.
- **Build Alliances:** Success is rarely a solo journey. Surround yourself with people who support and challenge you.
- **Own Your Authenticity:** Don't dilute your identity to fit others' expectations. Your uniqueness is your greatest strength.
- **Pay It Forward:** Leadership isn't just about climbing the ladder; it's about holding it steady for the next person.

■ ■ ■

Harpreet's journey proves that leadership isn't about fitting into a mold—it's about breaking it. It's about showing up as your whole self, refusing to shrink, and making room for others to do the same. In a world where the odds are stacked against us, part of our leadership—our legacy—is to take up space, to challenge the status quo, and to create real change.

I like to think of it as being the Rosa Parks of the Digital Age.

Sit at the front of the bus. Refuse to let outdated systems and long-standing biases decide your next move. Speak up, take action, and own your place at the table, as each of these women have done. Because when you do, you're not just making a move for yourself—you're opening doors for every woman coming up behind you. That's how change happens. That's how we rewrite the rules.

Chapter Recap

- The odds may not be in our favor, but it's up to us to challenge the status quo and take control of our own career growth.

- Getting promoted isn't just about hard work—it's about speaking up, making your ambitions known, and stepping into leadership with confidence and intention.

- Real leadership goes beyond personal success; it's about creating change and paving the way for those who come next.

Embracing the Journey

Start by reflecting on what truly matters to you and what fuels your passion. Identify your unique strengths, skills, and superpowers that you want to leverage further in your career, and let this be the foundation of your personal development plan. Writing this down will help you visualize and shape your vision more clearly.

Chapter 12

To Microsoft and Beyond

I believe innovation is the most powerful force for change in the world.

—Bill Gates

As we close this remarkable 50-year journey with the She, let's take a moment to honor the courage it took for her to step into the world of technology—not just to find a place, but to make it her own. She walked every road that led to Microsoft, and when she arrived, she didn't just step into rooms—she owned them. She didn't wait for permission. She claimed space in the rooms of the house and transformed it into a place of belonging, a home.

She stood up—not just for herself, but for every woman who would come after her. She made sure inclusion wasn't just a conversation, but a lived experience. She faced down biases, refused to be boxed in by outdated narratives, and took ownership of her story before anyone else could write it for her. She learned to laugh in the face of perfectionism, to burn bright without burning out, and to embrace lifelong learning as a source of power.

Over the last 50 years, the She has shaped technology—and let it shape her in return. It has been a powerful, symbiotic journey, bringing her to where she stands today. The She will tell you that with each breakthrough in technology, she, too, has experienced a personal milestone. With digital transformation also came personal transformation. Technology hasn't just been a space for her to step into—it has been a partner in her growth, a force that has evolved with her. Together, they have shaped each other, woven together by code and confidence. Jane Santos Stander, Senior Business Strategy Analyst, Americas, exemplifies this journey beautifully.

She the Unlabeled: A Journey to the Future and Beyond

Coming from a small town in Brazil to the United States has been a journey of tenacity—one that continues to teach me valuable lessons every day. It was with this same tenacity that I found my way to Microsoft nearly 20 years ago—almost by accident, though I believe nothing truly happens by accident.

I started at Microsoft creating customer support content in Brazilian Portuguese and Spanish for Latin America. At the time, my technical confidence was close to zero. Back then, candidates in the United States with professional language backgrounds from Latin America were scarce, and my language skills were more valued than my technical expertise. My interviewers must have seen potential in me—the Learn-Her-All mindset—and that's how I became a She.

Tech and the She Evolution

Eventually, I transitioned from managing language projects to collaborating with engineers on technical content for Latin America. I was not just learning new skills—I was redefining my own capabilities. Supporting mobile operators during the Windows Phone era pushed me out of my comfort zone, as I navigated a male-dominated tech environment and discovered resilience in the face of both professional challenges and personal doubts. When I returned to Brazil in 2014 to reconnect with my roots, I realized how much I had grown. My expertise was evolving, but my confidence lagged behind. Returning to the United States in 2017, I pursued localization engineering and eventually earned a master's in Information Systems. It was then that I finally recognized that every milestone at Microsoft mirrored a milestone in my own development—teaching me that transformation is a gradual process, and self-belief grows with every step forward.

The Future: She, the Unlabeled

The ability to learn new languages—whether spoken or coded—is a gift. I have been a translator, a cultural voyager, a teacher, a technologist, a wife, a mother, a daughter, and an explorer. And as technology continues to evolve, it offers us limitless potential.

A decade ago, voice recognition struggled to detect accents. Today, AI-powered Copilots interpret idioms, voice tones, and even facial expressions. The future of robotics, Dataverse, and AI-powered translation is unfolding before us.

What began as a job in translation became a lifelong passion for knowledge. It's not about what I have accomplished or what I have left behind—it's about what comes next.

Technology, as my partner in personal growth, has not only guided my aspirations, but inspired me to continue exploring a concept I'm calling *Unlabeled*. We are people of every color, parents and children, dreamers and builders. We all speak different languages—some of us more than one. Some of us are the She—women in tech, women at Microsoft. And all of us have something to share, to give, and to learn. Labels don't define us and neither do barriers.

■ ■ ■

As you can see, the She is stepping boldly into the next 50 years. She is ensuring that technology works for us, not the other way around. Just in the last three years, we've witnessed a surge of innovation—advancements in AI and machine learning, quantum computing, next-generation hardware, augmented and virtual reality, robotics, sustainable tech, and cybersecurity. And in the last two years alone, Microsoft has taken bold steps to expand its impact. Since announcing its partnership with OpenAI in 2023, we've seen an extraordinary acceleration of AI-powered solutions. The ability to engage with computers through natural conversation is no longer the future—it's happening right now. AI-powered voice and chatbots are generating content, drafting documents, composing music, and designing images with astonishing skill.

Agentic World

The next great leap—the one already unfolding—is the rise of the agentic world, where AI moves beyond simple assistance and begins actively managing complex tasks on our behalf. These AI agents will integrate seamlessly with systems, make decisions, and execute tasks, freeing us to focus on what matters most.

Imagine an AI agent that books your entire trip—checking your calendar, securing the best flights, coordinating hotel availability, and even factoring in local events to create an unforgettable experience. Now, scale that capability: an AI that plans a getaway for a group of friends, balancing multiple schedules, preferences, and budgets to find the perfect destination.

This is more than just convenience—it's a fundamental shift in how we engage with technology. AI agents will collaborate, problem-solve, and handle intricate processes that once required human intervention. And the opportunity here is enormous, particularly for women. This isn't just about efficiency; it's about reclaiming our time, energy, and creativity for the things that truly matter. With AI-driven solutions, women can gain confidence, develop new skills, and accelerate their independence—often without needing advanced technical knowledge or coding expertise.

Beyond skill-building, AI offers a transformative opportunity for women to improve their lives in multiple ways. Women juggle countless roles—as wives, mothers, daughters, professionals, friends, and leaders—constantly balancing personal and professional responsibilities. Yet, despite ongoing efforts to achieve gender parity, women continue to bear the brunt of household labor while working full-time jobs—even in the most progressive societies.

In the United States, women make up 57.5% of the workforce,[1] yet they spend twice as much time on household duties than their male counterparts.[2] In countries where workplace flexibility is limited or nonexistent, the burden is even greater. AI has the potential to ease these challenges, allowing women to reclaim their time and focus on what truly matters.

AI is becoming an everyday companion for women who learn to harness its power—not just to automate tasks but to empower ourselves. By offloading the mundane, they create space for innovation, leadership, and self-growth.

Satya Nadella once said, "AI is the defining technology of our times. It's augmenting human ingenuity and helping us solve some of society's most pressing challenges." Few are more ingenious than women when they uncover the right tools—not just to build themselves, but to uplift their families, communities, customers, and ultimately, entire societies. Freada Sylvester, Principal Program Manager, tells us how the She is experiencing this modern-day RenAIssance with her customers.

 The Modern Day RenAIssance

This is an incredible moment; one I've never experienced in my personal or professional lifetime until now. The possibilities in the Era of AI seem limitless, but the hyper-speed and hyperscale rate of change and innovation are pushing everyone to think and execute differently. What do I mean? Over the past two years, AI has become a household term, almost commoditized. Every organization I've encountered is scrambling to establish a point of view and plan for transforming with these new capabilities. Many conversations start with the "tech," AI, and work backward to find a problem it can solve. Over and over, I've had to pull the discussion back to basics and ask what challenges or opportunities are top of mind, putting tech aside.

Instead of starting from "I need to use AI to reduce my internal support costs," I spend hours getting stakeholders to reframe it to something like, "I need to find x% of efficiencies in internal support costs over the next 12 months." The difference between those two statements is light years, and the chance of successfully achieving one versus the other is even further apart. The former statement is limited by the tech, while the latter is open to all the possibilities that tech can provide.

Let's continue with this example. As we dig into proper discovery around what efficiencies the customer is interested in driving and for whom, what always surfaces is how much bigger the scenario and associated opportunity is than initially imagined. What appeared as a pure AI-powered search experience quickly morphs into search + retrieve + organize + generate + . . . it never fails!

I realized that most scenarios, once clearly articulated, could be categorized into a few archetypal behavior buckets:

1. **Show me.** The search and retrieve experience mentioned above. Find and organize something for me using natural language inputs and outputs with a clear understanding of the user's intent.

2. **Create for me.** Generate something like a document, text, visual, presentation, etc., based on an input that can include contextual information, i.e., an existing asset.

3. **Analyze for me.** Compare and contrast information, identify risks/gaps, provide insights around a thing or set of things.
4. **Do for me.** Take an action for me. This is where it gets really interesting.

Every scenario, every use case will tick one, some, or all of these buckets. The key is to quickly break down scenarios into the buckets and then leverage the tech stack, *a la* AI, to meet the needs. What emerges is a set of technology patterns you can repeatedly apply to these behaviors. Once you've built a "show me" + "create" experience, you have the beginnings of a framework you can codify and automate wherever the patterns appear.

Now that we've got the basics out of the way, what's next? Once customers realize these behavior buckets, the doors swing open, and the advanced possibilities begin to reveal themselves. Automated application of AI everywhere the behavior exists, automatic chaining of behaviors together with matching AI capabilities at runtime, predictive pattern matching—it's mind-blowing! The future is about every person having an AI Copilot and every process having an AI agent, but I'd take it a step further and say every behavior will have an AI action, too.

■ ■ ■

If this is true, then the possibilities for integrating AI technology are endless. As we look toward the future of designing this technology, Sogol Malekzadeh, Partner Design Director, reminds us that with these possibilities also come important responsibilities.

The Art of the Possible with AI

AI holds endless possibilities, not just as a tool, but as a partner in shaping a better future. Right now, we have the opportunity to design AI in ways that improve lives, helping people achieve their diverse goals and aspirations. AI has the potential to create more inclusive, meaningful, and thoughtful products, breaking down barriers and expanding opportunities for all. It's up to us to guide its development, ensuring that AI adapts to human needs rather than the other way around. I see AI as a collaborator—one that enhances creativity, expands capabilities, and takes on repetitive tasks so that we can focus on innovation and impact. It's like having an extra set of hands, freeing us to explore new possibilities in both our professional and personal lives.

Agent-based, multimodal AI systems are becoming an integral part of our daily experiences, offering more intuitive and contextual interactions. Imagine AI that doesn't just process words but perceives emotions, actions, and environments, responding with insights that truly align with our needs. Grounding AI within real-world contexts allows for more meaningful actions and interactions, making technology feel less like a tool and more like an intelligent partner. This shift has become increasingly evident over the past decade, as advancements in human-AI collaboration have demonstrated AI's ability to transform complex data into compelling narratives, maximizing both automation and human agency. The goal isn't to replace human creativity but to enhance it, making collaboration between people and AI more productive and empowering.

Think about a world where products and experiences adapt effortlessly to individual needs—where people of all abilities can seamlessly interact with technology because AI anticipates and adjusts to them. Empathy and understanding are at the heart of great design, and AI offers the potential to create deeply personalized experiences that elevate and empower. As designers, leaders, and innovators, we are not just witnessing this evolution; we are shaping it. AI will change how we work, think, and create, pushing us to develop better products and services that help people succeed in their jobs and beyond.

But we must ensure we drive what we call Responsible AI at Microsoft. As we develop and deploy AI, we must prioritize ethics, transparency, and inclusivity. AI must be designed to minimize biases, leveraging human feedback and external knowledge to ensure fairness and accuracy. Trust is the foundation of innovation, and by embedding these principles into AI, we can create systems that genuinely serve the common good. The future of AI must be built on collaboration, curiosity, and a shared commitment to creating technology that respects and enhances human values. AI should not replace human ingenuity—it should amplify it. By combining human insight with AI's capabilities, we can build solutions that uplift, empower, and inspire us to work and play.

■ ■ ■

AI in Gaming

Speaking of play, think about how AI is revolutionizing gaming—creating entirely new worlds and transforming how we play, and reshaping the industry itself. Sarah Bond, President of XBOX, shares with us how AI is redefining what's possible in gaming.

The Future of Gaming with AI

The powerful thing about gaming is its ability to create shared experiences and develop empathy between people. Games deepen our understanding of each other, inspiring us to forge connections, experience joy, and stretch our imaginations—which is why we believe in enabling more people to play more games more easily.

AI will accelerate that by amplifying human ingenuity. Games have long leveraged AI for that exact purpose—from enhancing storytelling with intelligent non-playable characters (NPCs) and dynamically aware opponents, to simulating real-world weather patterns, to interpreting complex physics. As AI advances, we see new opportunities opening up for game creators to explore innovations in design, development, and discovery—and we can't wait to see what they build next.

■ ■ ■

Responsible AI

Responsible AI isn't just about pushing the boundaries of technology—it's about trust, security, and the basic human right to feel safe, both online and in the real world. And for women, safety is never an afterthought. It's a daily negotiation, a constant calculation. We carry our keys between our fingers when we walk alone at night. We think twice before sharing personal details online. We adapt to a world that was not built with our safety in mind.

In the digital age, these risks have only grown. The threats women face aren't just physical—they are woven into the very technologies we rely on. AI-driven deepfakes are weaponized to harass and humiliate. Personal data is exploited to stalk and control. Biased algorithms fail to protect women from online abuse, financial fraud, and misinformation. And in many parts of the world, digital surveillance is used as a tool of oppression, limiting women's freedoms rather than expanding them. AI has the power to drive progress, but only if it is designed responsibly. That means ensuring women have a seat at the table—so that technology doesn't just serve half the population, but protects and empowers all of us.

At Microsoft, trust is not just a goal—it's a responsibility. And it rests on three core pillars: the Secure Future Initiative, Responsible AI, and unwavering commitments to privacy. These principles guide every innovation, ensuring that technology is not only powerful but also ethical, inclusive, and resilient. The stakes have never been higher. AI is transforming our world at an unprecedented pace, and with that transformation comes both promise and risk. But with strategic innovation, responsible leadership, and collective action, we have an opportunity—to build a future where security isn't an afterthought, but a guarantee.

Leave No One Behind

Another powerful tool for protection is education—because understanding AI and its impact is essential to navigating this new era with confidence. As we explored in Chapter 9, we don't just have a right to shape the AI revolution—we have a responsibility. Ensuring that AI remains accessible and equitable for all is one of the greatest challenges of our time.

Lucia Rodrigues, AI National Skills Director Brazil, offers invaluable insights on why AI literacy matters and how it is already transforming lives across Brazil.

Connect AI

When I first learned about artificial intelligence and its potential to transform lives at scale, I was both fascinated and determined. The question wasn't just how AI could be developed, but how it could be made accessible to everyone—especially in a country as vast and diverse as Brazil. That challenge became the foundation of the National AI Skilling Program, an ambitious initiative aimed at ensuring AI reaches and empowers every individual, regardless of background or resources.

My name is Lucia Rodrigues, and I lead this initiative at Microsoft Brazil. We have 230 million recipients in our program, which we call Connect AI. Our mission is simple: To make AI accessible to all and equip people with the skills they need to improve their lives. AI has the power to generate economic opportunities, but digital literacy remains a major barrier, particularly in a country where access to computers is limited. With less than 30% of Brazilians owning a computer, smartphones have become the primary tool for digital inclusion. This reality shaped our strategy, allowing us to meet people where they are—on their mobile devices.

We designed the program to serve key audiences: government workers, non-profit employees, teachers, students, and job seekers. Each group faces unique challenges but shares a common goal of enhancing their capabilities through AI. One of our first breakthroughs was a partnership with the Ministry of Labor to create a digital school, offering courses on everything from basic digital literacy to advanced AI skills. Today, more than 1.7 million people actively learn through this platform, gaining knowledge that empowers them to navigate the evolving digital world.

Government workers were a critical focus, as Brazil's public sector employs more than four million people. By integrating AI fluency courses into the digital school, we upskilled 60,000 government employees in just one year. Enhancing their productivity has had a ripple effect, improving the efficiency and effectiveness of public services across the country.

Another priority was equipping teachers with AI tools to help them manage large classrooms and limited resources. Brazil faces a severe teacher shortage, and many educators are overwhelmed by administrative tasks that take time away from teaching. We partnered with Nova Scala, a non-profit, to create content that helps teachers use AI for lesson planning, test creation, and administrative work. A task that once took an hour—such as preparing a Greek history exam for fourth graders—can now be done in just 10 minutes with AI assistance. This shift allows teachers to focus on what only they can do: engaging students, fostering critical thinking, and creating meaningful learning experiences.

For students, AI offers new opportunities to bridge gaps in education. Brazil's school system struggles with accessibility and quality, leaving many students without the resources they need. Through our program, we provide AI tools that assist with research, exam preparation, and even language learning. One of my mentees, for example, is using AI to teach herself Korean—a skill she once thought was out of reach. AI is not just enhancing education; it's expanding students' horizons and opening doors to new possibilities.

Job seekers are another key audience, as Brazil's unemployment rate remains high, and many people lack the digital skills required in today's job market. We teach participants how to use AI for resume building, job interview preparation, and career exploration. AI can simulate interview scenarios, provide real-time feedback, and help job seekers improve their skills, making them more competitive in the workforce.

One of the most inspiring aspects of this initiative is seeing its tangible impact. Every week, we send AI skill-building tips to 40 million people through a government app, encouraging them to explore AI and integrate it into their daily lives. The response has been incredible—millions are actively engaging, learning, and using AI to enhance their work, education, and opportunities.

We understand that AI literacy isn't just about learning new tools—it's about understanding their ethical implications. We emphasize critical thinking, teaching participants how to verify information, question sources, and recognize bias in AI-generated content. In an age of misinformation, these skills are just as crucial as technical proficiency.

As we continue to expand the National AI Skilling Program, I feel an incredible sense of urgency and optimism. Generative AI technology is moving fast, and we must act just as quickly to ensure that no one is left behind. The future of AI shouldn't be limited to those with access to cutting-edge technology—it should be a tool for everyone, helping people build better futures for themselves, their families, and their communities.

■ ■ ■

The next five years will bring advancements that push these innovations beyond anything we've seen before—not just recognizing patterns but demonstrating real intelligence. AI will evolve with memory, reasoning, and planning—systems that don't just process information but truly understand, anticipate, and adapt. Robotics will advance alongside AI, becoming more intuitive and capable of learning from experience, adjusting to new situations, and collaborating naturally with humans. The next generation of Large Language Models (LLMs) will move beyond predicting text to developing memory, common sense, and reasoning, enabling AI to build real mental models of the world and understand context, intent, and deeper meaning. But perhaps the most transformative breakthrough on the horizon is quantum computing. We are on the brink of a revolution in quantum algorithms, security, and real-world applications that could redefine entire industries. In finance and cybersecurity, quantum encryption will make our digital world more secure, while AI-driven financial models will create smarter, more resilient economies. In pharmaceuticals, AI and quantum computing will accelerate drug discovery, reducing the time and cost of developing life-saving treatments. In materials science, we will be able to design stronger, lighter, and more sustainable materials at the molecular level.

Ester de Nicolas Bonito, Senior Director, Quantum and AI for Science, shares her vision of the near future and the transformative potential of quantum computing.

Understanding the Language of Nature

Imagine a world where we can communicate directly with nature itself—where we use the language of chemistry and physics to unlock discoveries we never thought possible. That's the future I see, and it will be made real with quantum computing.

But before we look forward, let's take a step back. Science, at its core, hasn't changed all that much over the centuries. The way we make breakthroughs has remained largely the same. Scientists begin with a hypothesis, shaped by their knowledge and experience. They then run simulations—often using powerful supercomputers—to solve complex equations that describe physical and chemical processes. If a promising candidate emerges, it moves to laboratory testing, but this is where progress slows. Many candidates fail, and each cycle of refinement can take years, even decades. This is especially true in fields like pharmaceuticals, where bringing a new drug to market is both time-intensive and extraordinarily expensive.

But what if we could change that? What if we could reimagine the scientific process using AI and quantum computing—not just as tools, but as partners in discovery?

Teaching AI the Language of Nature

Right now, we're making huge strides in training AI to understand language, breaking it down into vectors and relationships between words. But what if, instead of focusing on human language, we applied this to chemistry—the fundamental language of nature?

By building foundational AI models that can interpret chemical and physical processes, we're unlocking a whole new way to reason about the natural world. This is a game-changer. Just as modern AI breakthroughs depend on advances in GPUs and computing power, the next evolution of AI will require even more sophisticated infrastructure to process, learn, and generate insights.

AI as a Catalyst for Scientific Discovery

Generative AI isn't just for writing emails or creating presentations—it's on the brink of transforming how we make scientific discoveries. Instead of relying on manually sifting through data, AI can work with scientists to generate millions of hypotheses, each grounded in scientific principles. Take the search for new materials as an example. In a recent study to find a better electrolyte for batteries, an AI model initially generated 32 million possible candidates. That's an unimaginable number for any human to process—it would take lifetimes. But specialized AI models can filter these candidates, applying criteria like synthesizability, supply chain availability, toxicity, and regulatory compliance. This narrows the list to the most promising possibilities, making scientific breakthroughs faster and more efficient than ever before.

The Ultimate Enabler

One of the most exciting aspects of this vision is the integration of quantum computing. Unlike traditional computers, which struggle to simulate complex molecules due to the immense computational demands, quantum computers operate using the same principles that govern the natural world. This makes them uniquely suited to tackling problems that are currently unsolvable.

Imagine replacing years of trial and error with precise, near-perfect quantum simulations. Instead of spending millions of dollars on lab experiments, we could use quantum computing to identify the most viable solutions in a fraction of the time.

- In drug discovery, quantum simulations could pinpoint the most promising molecular structures, dramatically reducing the cost and time needed to develop new medications.
- In agriculture, quantum computing could help design more sustainable fertilizers, boosting crop yields while minimizing environmental harm.
- In climate science, quantum systems could optimize CO_2 capture methods, accelerating the fight against climate change.

These aren't just theoretical ideas—they're within reach. But for this to work, we need a seamless integration of AI, supercomputing, and quantum technologies. When these systems work together, they not only speed up discoveries but also generate better data—which in turn improves AI models, creating a cycle of continuous progress.

Democratizing Science for All

One of the most powerful aspects of this technological shift is its potential to democratize scientific discovery. By making these advanced tools accessible—not just to top research institutions, but to scientists, students, and innovators everywhere—we can empower more minds to tackle the world's biggest challenges.

The goal is to remove the barriers to discovery. Instead of scientists spending time managing IT infrastructure, they can focus on solving real problems. Imagine a future where a high school student can run AI-powered experiments, or where small research teams can make breakthroughs that once required billion-dollar labs.

A Future Limited Only by Our Imagination

I believe we are standing at the edge of something extraordinary—a new era of discovery where AI and quantum computing are not just tools but catalysts for change. We have the opportunity to fundamentally reshape industries, improve lives, and create a more sustainable and equitable world.

This isn't just speculation. It's happening now. And the possibilities? They are as limitless as our curiosity, creativity, and courage to explore them.

■ ■ ■

Hello, World!

The possibilities before us are vast, and the excitement about what's ahead is undeniable. Brad Smith, President of Microsoft, has compared this moment to something even bigger than the Industrial Revolution. I think about the women of that era—stepping onto a steam-powered train for the first time or placing their first call over a newly invented telephone. It must have felt exhilarating, and maybe a little daunting. I'd like to believe that every major technological breakthrough has ultimately served one fundamental purpose: human connection. It is both our right and our deepest desire to be part of something greater than ourselves—to learn from one another, to share, to connect. Community is at the heart of who we are. And few understand the power of community better than Heather Cook, Principal Program Manager, Microsoft 365 Customer Advocacy and Community Engagement, who will share the final story in this book.

Code, Confidence, and Community

The future for women—at Microsoft and beyond—rests on the strength of our relationships, the resilience of our communities, and our unwavering commitment to our core values. Technology will continue to evolve, with AI driving new efficiencies and automating the repetitive, just as the Cloud transformed the way we work. But our success isn't just about embracing innovation—it's about maintaining the human connections that give us confidence, support, and a sense of belonging.

For me, connection has always been at the heart of everything I do. My career has been about creating experiences for others, fueled by a deep curiosity for technology and a passion for building meaningful relationships—especially among women. I see a future where we, as women, continue to stand together, amplify each other's voices, and lift as we climb. The next 50 years are ours to shape, and by fostering strong communities, we can ensure that the world ahead is not just one of possibility, but of purpose.

Of course, the road hasn't always been easy. Like so many women, I've faced triumphs and challenges alike—difficult managers, workplace politics, and moments of gaslighting, gatekeeping, and ghosting. But through it all, I have leaned on the power of relationships. A friend once gave me advice that has guided me through my career: in any situation, you have three choices—love it, leave it, or lump it (accept it as it is). At different points, I've navigated all three. But one truth has always remained: you never know who will be your advocate, who will open a door for you, or who will have your back when you need an ally. Keeping those relationships strong—staying connected—is the key to long-term success.

If you had asked me 30 years ago, fresh out of the University of Washington's School of Drama, what I thought my future would hold, I never would have imagined spending nearly 25 years working in and around the largest tech company in the world. I had dreams of performing—perhaps as a singer like Bette Midler or Liza Minnelli, or as a radio host like Graham Norton. But my journey took an unexpected turn when I found myself designing posters and marketing for my Seattle fringe theatre company. That creative work led me into the tech world when, during the dot-com bust, a friend's spouse introduced me to an opportunity in Microsoft's newly launched SharePoint division.

One conversation changed everything—my first role as a Microsoft vendor sparked years of staying curious and learning from every person I met. I transformed my background as a theatre producer into a global event producer, helping produce major Microsoft events like TechEd Barcelona, Microsoft Build, and Ignite, while the SharePoint community became my home, filled with relationships that spanned continents and shaped my career. By 2011, I was a marketing executive, Microsoft MVP, startup founder, and podcast host, speaking at 28 events across four continents in 2019. When the COVID-19 pandemic hit, live events vanished, but once again, community saved the day—Karuana Gatimu called me to help transition Microsoft's flagship events online, and together we built the Virtual Event Playbook, moving MVP Summit and Build to digital platforms in record time. Later that year, Dona Sarkar led me to a new role, heading the Power Platform community, bringing me back to my SharePoint roots and the power of vibrant, engaged networks. I helped launch the Microsoft Power Platform Community Conference, one of the largest post-pandemic in-person events, and returned to the Microsoft 365 Customer Advocacy Team under Jeff Teper—the same leader I worked with more than two decades ago when my journey in tech first began.

Looking back, every chapter of my journey has been shaped by the people around me—mentors, colleagues, allies, and friends. The Microsoft community is a giant melting pot of passionate, diverse individuals, each bringing their own expertise, creativity, and energy. Some love their Microsoft 365 Minestrone, others prefer SQL Server Stew or Windows Bisque—but at the end of the day, we are all part of something bigger than ourselves. We share knowledge, lift each other up, and create opportunities together.

■ ■ ■

The future of technology, the workforce, and women will never be defined by tools alone. It will always come back to people—the communities we nurture, the voices we amplify, and the connections that empower us. Over the past 50 years, women—the She—at

Microsoft have been at the heart of technological progress. Alongside the 27.6% of women in the tech industry,[3] we've built, shaped, and coded the innovations that power our world today. And the future holds even greater promises. In just the next 5 years, we're expected to see a net increase of 78 million jobs globally,[4] with technology, data, and AI roles leading the way. I can only imagine what the next 50 years will bring.

If history has taught us anything, it's that women in tech won't just carve out a place for themselves—they'll build something extraordinary. The last 50 years have equipped us with not only the technical skills but the courage, community, and compassion to lead. The future is bright with possibility, and I believe that the She and also we—you, me, our daughters, and their daughters—will not just thrive in this evolving landscape. We will lead with grace and purpose, reigning sovereign in a world we've helped to create, driven by code and confidence.

Chapter Recap

- Over the past 50 years, technology and the women in the industry have grown together, transforming one another in powerful, lasting ways.

- As technology advances, women are leveraging innovation not just to build new skills and reclaim their time, but to shape their own personal and professional growth.

- The Era of AI offers women a unique chance to lead, using technology as a tool to drive equity, equality, and meaningful change in the world.

> **Inspiration for the Journey**
>
> Seek out communities and workplaces that inspire and uplift you. Surround yourself with people who fuel your growth and share in your vision. These connections will serve as your foundation as you navigate the ever-evolving landscape of technology—and thrive within it.

Chapter 13

Portrait Gallery

AJA HILL | DIRECTOR OF CLOUD SOLUTION ARCHITECTS AND WOMEN CHAPTER WW CO-CHAIR

Representation matters, and I believe deeply in its power to transform lives and shape a better world.

ANNE-CLAIRE (AC) LO BIANCO | SENIOR PARTNER AND PROGRAM DEVELOPMENT MANAGER, MICROSOFT FOR STARTUPS

It's extremely scary to put myself out there, but here I am.

CARISSA ROUSE | DIRECTOR

To find your most authentic self, you also have to find out who you are not.

DÉBORA DI PIANO | DIGITAL NATIVE ACCOUNT EXECUTIVE

Microsoft isn't just a company to me—it's a part of my story, a place where I've grown, stumbled, and succeeded.

DIANE C. BOETTCHER | DIRECTOR OF BUSINESS MANAGEMENT, INDUSTRY SOLUTIONS DELIVERY, AMERICAS

Laughter and letting go are powerful antidotes to the pressure of perfection.

DONA SARKAR

If you were going to fit into that nice, neat box in your company, you probably would have done it by now.

ESTER DE NICOLAS BONITO | SENIOR DIRECTOR, QUANTUM AND AI FOR SCIENCE

We are standing at the edge of something extraordinary—a new era of discovery where AI and quantum computing are not just tools but catalysts for change.

FREADA SYLVESTER | PRINCIPAL PROGRAM MANAGER

The future is about every person having an AI Copilot and every process having an AI agent.

GABRIELLA JOO | GROUP FINANCE MANAGER

I never planned or intended to work at Microsoft, but it has turned into a very rewarding journey.

GARIMA GAURAV | SENIOR PROGRAM MANAGER

I was the first woman in my family to step beyond the boundaries of my state—and eventually my country—to follow my dreams.

GINNIEE SAHI | FORMER GLOBAL ACCOUNTS LEADER

If the right space doesn't exist, create one. Build a place where diversity and creativity are not just welcomed, but celebrated.

HAPREET KAPOUR | PRINCIPAL TECHNICAL PROGRAM MANAGER

Advocate for yourself: Speak up for your achievements and your worth—because no one else will do it for you.

HEATHER COOK | PRINCIPAL PROGRAM MANAGER, MICROSOFT 365 CUSTOMER ADVOCACY, COMMUNITY ENGAGEMENT

Through it all, I have leaned on the power of relationships.

IMANE EL MAJDOUBI | ENTERPRISE COMMERCIAL LEAD UAE

I've always believed that when I'm fulfilled professionally, I'm a better mother.

JANE SANTOS STANDER | SENIOR BUSINESS STRATEGY ANALYST, AMERICAS

Labels don't define us and neither do barriers.

JENIA FULTON | LOGISTICS TECHNICIAN

Despite not having a tech background, I decided to apply.

JENNIFER COOPER | FORMER MICROSOFT DEI LEADER AND CHIEF OF STAFF

Sometimes, breaking the rules is exactly what's needed.

KASIA STAŃCZAK | SENIOR TECHNICAL RECRUITER

My journey from the meat industry to tech is proof that with the right mindset and determination, you can carve a path that aligns with your dream.

LAIBA A. KHAN | ENTERPRISE SUCCESS MANAGER

Every win and challenge has been accompanied by impactful mentors and teachable moments.

LAN YE | CVP TEAMS ENGINEERING

Looking to the future with AI, I see immense opportunities for enhancing productivity and collaboration within Microsoft Teams.

LISANNE BRONS | GLOBAL BLACK BELT M365 COPILOT

Go ahead, underestimate me . . . I'll show you what I've got.

LUCIA RODRIGUES | AI NATIONAL SKILLS DIRECTOR BRAZIL

AI literacy isn't just about learning new tools—it's about understanding their ethical implications.

MARIA MAALI | SENIOR BUSINESS DEVELOPMENT MANAGER AFRICA

The journey from a small startup to a thriving enterprise is one of the most inspiring parts of what we do.

MARISELA CERDA | DIRECTOR AZURE BUSINESS PROGRAM MANAGEMENT

The climb to leadership isn't about waiting for permission or hoping to be seen. It's about showing up, speaking your truth, and refusing to let the system tell you what you're capable of.

MARY SNAPP | VP, STRATEGIC INITIATIVES

Confidence isn't about knowing all the answers—it's about knowing that you have the strength to find them.

MELISSA LUONGO | HR DIRECTOR CENTRAL EUROPE

People are such an integral part of any technology business, and fostering that connection is at the heart of what I do.

MICHELLE MARKHAM | ANZ K-12 EDUCATION DIRECTOR

Confidence isn't something you're born with; it's something you build, one step at a time.

MONALISA SENGUPTA | PARTNER DIRECTOR OF PM, COPILOT AGENTS AND TEAMS ECOSYSTEM

I've never walked into a room thinking of myself as a woman leader. I've always walked in as someone ready to deliver.

Portrait Gallery

NATALIA NIKONENKO | SENIOR TECHNICAL SPECIALIST
Rarely do we turn the lens inward to examine the biases we hold about ourselves. Yet, these internal biases can be the most damaging.

NATALIIA BURLAKOVA | SENIOR SPECIALIST
Before the war, my favorite quote was, 'What doesn't kill us makes us stronger.' Not anymore.

NA-YOUNG CHOI | CHIEF OF STAFF
Early in my career, I discovered the value of adapting, learning smartly, and bringing my own unique contributions to the table.

OKSANA MALESHYKHINA | SENIOR TECHNICAL SPECIALIST
For years, I believed perfectionism was my superpower. But it was dragging me down, not lifting me up.

POOJA SUND | PRINCIPAL PM MANAGER
Be bold. Be brave. Be you.

PURNA VIRJI | PRINCIPAL CONTENT SOLUTIONS CONSULTANT AT LINKEDIN
To teach is to learn twice.

DR. RENATE STRAZDINA, D.SC. | NATIONAL TECHNOLOGY OFFICER CENTRAL EUROPE

Continuous learning is vital—not just for personal growth, but for adapting to a constantly changing world.

RITA ROBBINS | AI AND EXECUTIVE SPEAKING COACH

Be bold: Don't wait for someone else to fix the problem. Your boldness could be the catalyst for change.

SARAH BOND | PRESIDENT OF XBOX

Gaming is a unique art form, with no single formula for success.

SARAH MOCKE | VICE PRESIDENT, ENGINEERING & ARCHITECTURE

Knowing what brings you joy and aligns with your strengths is the foundation of effective leadership.

SARKA KOHOUTOVA | SENIOR BUSINESS PROGRAM MANAGER

In the end, diversity and inclusion are not just about ticking boxes; they are about creating a world where everyone has the opportunity to thrive.

SHAKENA BEEMAN | SENIOR PROGRAM MANAGER

Every experience—good or bad—has made me who I am.

SHIRA FAYANS BIRENBAUM | FORMER COO & CMO MICROSOFT ISRAEL

The Bias Monster isn't always a villain to be slain—it's often a reminder of the work still left to do.

SOGOL MALEKZADEH | PARTNER DESIGN DIRECTOR

Trust is the foundation of innovation, and by embedding ethics, transparency, and inclusivity into AI, we can create systems that genuinely serve the common good.

SONIA CUFF | PRINCIPAL CLOUD ADVOCATE LEAD

Sometimes the most productive thing you can do is step back and recharge.

SONIA WADHWA | SENIOR DIRECTOR

My biases nearly deprived me of a fulfilling career and personal growth.

STACY TATEM | FORMER SOLUTION SPECIALIST

Looking back on my career, one principle has guided me: the power of being a learn-it-all.

STEPH BURG | PRINCIPAL DIRECTOR OF ENGINEERING

I've learned to embrace the unexpected, trust my instincts, and follow my dreams wherever they lead.

SUSIE KANDZOR | SENIOR DIRECTOR OF HACKING IN THE GARAGE AT MICROSOFT

Fostering a culture of innovation where everyone feels included is the key to sustained success.

VASU JAKKAL | CVP SECURITY

Dare greatly.

WENDY WANG | SENIOR SOFTWARE ENGINEER

Life isn't about choosing between your passions and responsibilities—it's about finding harmony between them.

WERONIKA SKOWERA | CUSTOMER SUCCESS ACCOUNT MANAGER

Sometimes, the greatest motivation comes from those who doubt us the most.

Notes

Chapter 1

1. WomenTech Network. "What Barriers Do Women Face in Tech and How Can We Overcome Them?" Accessed January 31, 2025. https://www.womentech.net/en-us/how-to/what-barriers-do-women-face-in-tech-and-how-can-we-overcome-them.
2. Gates, Bill. "It's fine to celebrate success but it is more important to heed the lessons of failure." *BrainyQuote.com.* Accessed January 31, 2025. https://www.brainyquote.com/quotes/bill_gates_385735.
3. Coffman, Katherine B. "How Gender Stereotypes Kill a Woman's Self-Confidence." *Harvard Business School Working Knowledge*, December 17, 2018. Accessed January 31, 2025. https://www.library.hbs.edu/working-knowledge/how-gender-stereotypes-less-than-br-greater-than-kill-a-woman-s-less-than-br-greater-than-self-confidence.
4. Ballard Brief. "The Link Between Social Media and Body Image Issues Among Youth in the United States." Accessed January 31, 2025. https://ballardbrief.byu.edu/issue-briefs/the-link-between-social-media-and-body-image-issues-among-youth-in-the-united-states.
5. American Psychological Association. "Social Media and Body Image." Accessed January 31, 2025. https://www.apa.org/news/press/releases/2023/02/social-media-body-image.
6. Harvard Graduate School of Education. "Social Media and Teen Anxiety." *Usable Knowledge.* Accessed January 31, 2025. https://www.gse.harvard.edu/ideas/usable-knowledge/17/12/social-media-and-teen-anxiety.

7. Pew Research Center. "The Enduring Grip of the Gender Pay Gap." March 1, 2023. Accessed January 31, 2025. https://www.pewresearch.org/social-trends/2023/03/01/the-enduring-grip-of-the-gender-pay-gap/.
8. World Economic Forum. "Global Gender Gap Report 2024." Accessed January 31, 2025. https://www.weforum.org/publications/global-gender-gap-report-2024/digest.

Chapter 2

1. World Economic Forum. "The Reskilling Revolution: Better Skills, Better Jobs, Better Education for a Billion People by 2030." *World Economic Forum*, January 22, 2020. Accessed January 31, 2025. https://www.weforum.org/press/2020/01/the-reskilling-revolution-better-skills-better-jobs-better-education-for-a-billion-people-by-2030/.
2. World Economic Forum. "Jobs of Tomorrow: Mapping Opportunity in the New Economy." *World Economic Forum*, January 2020. Accessed January 31, 2025. https://www.weforum.org/publications/jobs-of-tomorrow-mapping-opportunity-in-the-new-economy/.
3. Goldfarb, Avi, Ryan C. McDevitt, and Catherine Tucker. "The Early Adoption of Generative AI: Who, What, and Why?" Working Paper No. 32966. National Bureau of Economic Research, 2024. Accessed January 31, 2025. https://www.nber.org/papers/w32966.
4. Deloitte. "Women and Generative AI: Closing the Gender Gap in Adoption and Use." *Deloitte Insights*, 2024. Accessed January 31, 2025. https://www2.deloitte.com/us/en/insights/industry/technology/technology-media-and-telecom-predictions/2025/women-and-generative-ai.html.

Chapter 3

1. Portable Press. "What It Cost in 1980." Portable Press, May 6, 2015. Accessed January 31, 2025. https://www.portablepress.com/blog/2015/05/what-it-cost-in-1980/.
2. Inman. "Barbie's Malibu DreamHouse Would Command $10M—If It Was Real." *Inman*, July 21, 2023. Accessed January 31, 2025. https://www

.inman.com/2023/07/21/barbies-malibu-dreamhouse-would-command-10m-if-it-was-real/.
3. Ochs, Elinor, and Merav Shohet. "The Cultural Structuring of Mealtime Socialization." *New Directions for Child and Adolescent Development* 2006, no. 111 (2006): 35–49. Accessed January 31, 2025. https://doi.org/10.1002/cd.155.
4. University of Oxford. "Social Eating Connects Communities." University of Oxford News, March 16, 2017. Accessed January 31, 2025. https://www.ox.ac.uk/news/2017-03-16-social-eating-connects-communities.
5. Goldfarb, Avi, Ryan C. McDevitt, and Catherine Tucker. "The Early Adoption of Generative AI: Who, What, and Why?" Working Paper No. 32966. National Bureau of Economic Research, 2024. Accessed January 31, 2025. https://www.nber.org/papers/w32966.
6. Deloitte. "Women and Generative AI: Closing the Gender Gap in Adoption and Use." Deloitte Insights, 2024. Accessed January 31, 2025. https://www2.deloitte.com/us/en/insights/industry/technology/technology-media-and-telecom-predictions/2025/women-and-generative-ai.html.

Chapter 4

1. Kiradoo, Giriraj. "Diversity, Equity, and Inclusion in the Workplace: Strategies for Achieving and Sustaining a Diverse Workforce." SSRN, December 20, 2022. Accessed January 31, 2025. https://papers.ssrn.com/sol3/papers.cfm?abstract_id=4392136.
2. Coleman, L. Ray, and Erica D. Taylor. "The Importance of Diversity, Equity, and Inclusion for Effective, Ethical Leadership." *Clinics in Sports Medicine* 42, no. 2 (April 2023): 269–280. Accessed January 31, 2025. https://www.sportsmed.theclinics.com/article/S0278-5919(22)00092-8/fulltext.
3. HR Future. "Retreating from DEI Initiatives Could Cost Businesses Billions." *HR Future*, January 31, 2025. Accessed January 31, 2025. https://www.hrfuture.net/workplace-culture/diversity-equity-inclusion/retreating-from-dei-initiatives-could-cost-businesses-billions/.

4. Buildremote. "Report: 48 Organizations Cut or Ended DEI Since 2023." *Buildremote*, January 31, 2025. Accessed January 31, 2025. https://buildremote.com/report-48-organizations-cut-or-ended-dei-since-2023/.
5. Miller, Stephen. "Pursuing DEI in Europe's Workplaces Takes Different Route Than U.S." SHRM, January 31, 2025. Accessed January 31, 2025. https://www.shrm.org/resourcesandtools/hr-topics/global-hr/pages/pursuing-dei-in-europe-workplaces.aspx.
6. HRD Asia. "Why the West Has a Lot to Learn from Asia's Diversity and Inclusion." *HRD Asia*, January 31, 2025. Accessed January 31, 2025. https://www.hcamag.com/asia/specialisation/diversity-inclusion/why-the-west-has-a-lot-to-learn-from-asias-diversity-and-inclusion/319486.
7. Chambers and Partners. "DEI Trends in Asia-Pacific 2025 Guide." Chambers APAC Legal Topics, January 31, 2025. Accessed January 31, 2025. https://chambers.com/legal-trends/dei-trends-in-asia-pacific-2025-guide.
8. Africa, Diversity, Equity and Inclusion Forums. "Africa, Diversity, Equity and Inclusion Forums" *Africa, Diversity, Equity and Inclusion Forums*, January 31, 2025. Accessed January 31, 2025. https://www.africadeiforums.com/.
9. HR Policy Association. "DEI Challenges in Latin America – Things to Consider." *HR* Policy, January 31, 2025. Accessed January 31, 2025. https://www.hrpolicy.org/insight-and-research/dei-challenges-in-latin-america-things-to-consider/.
10. Microsoft. "Microsoft's 2024 Global Diversity & Inclusion Report: Our Most Global, Transparent Report Yet." Microsoft Official Blog, October 23, 2024. Accessed January 31, 2025. https://blogs.microsoft.com/blog/2024/10/23/microsofts-2024-global-diversity-inclusion-report-our-most-global-transparent-report-yet/.

Chapter 6

1. GeoStat.org. "Nationalities in Miami, Florida." Accessed January 31, 2025. https://www.geostat.org/data/miami-fl/nationality.

Chapter 7

1. Royal Swedish Academy of Sciences. *The Sveriges Riksbank Prize in Economic Sciences in Memory of Alfred Nobel 2023*. Stockholm: Royal Swedish Academy of Sciences, 2023. Accessed January 31, 2025. https://www.nobel prize.org/uploads/2023/10/popular-economicsciencesprize2023.pdf.

Chapter 9

1. World Economic Forum. *The Future of Jobs Report 2025*. Geneva: World Economic Forum, 2025. Accessed January 31, 2025. https://www.weforum.org/publications/the-future-of-jobs-report-2025/digest/.
2. Microsoft News Center. "Microsoft Launches Next Stage of Skills Initiative After Helping 30 Million People." *Microsoft*, March 30, 2021. Accessed January 31, 2025. https://news.microsoft.com/skills/.
3. Microsoft Learn. "Microsoft Azure AI Fundamentals: Generative AI." Accessed January 31, 2025. https://learn.microsoft.com/en-us/training/paths/azure-ai-fundamentals-generative-ai/.
4. Microsoft Learn. "Microsoft Certified: Azure AI Fundamentals." Accessed January 31, 2025. https://learn.microsoft.com/en-us/certifications/azure-ai-fundamentals/.
5. Microsoft Learn. "Develop Natural Language Processing Solutions with Azure AI Services AI-3003." Accessed January 31, 2025. https://learn.microsoft.com/en-us/training/modules/develop-nlp-solutions-azure-ai-services/.
6. LinkedIn Learning. "Streamlining Your Work with Microsoft Bing Chat." Accessed January 31, 2025. https://www.linkedin.com/learning/streamlining-your-work-with-microsoft-bing-chat.
7. Microsoft Learn. "Embrace Responsible AI Principles and Practices." Accessed January 31, 2025. https://learn.microsoft.com/en-us/training/modules/responsible-ai-principles/.

Chapter 10

1. Thompson, Julie. "5 Feminine Traits That Make Leaders Great." *Business.com*, January 31, 2025. Accessed January 31, 2025. https://www.business.com/articles/feminine-traits-for-leaders/.

Chapter 11

1. UN Women. Forecasting Women in Leadership Positions. New York: UN Women, 2023. Accessed January 31, 2025. https://www.unwomen.org/sites/default/files/2023-11/forecasting-women-in-leadership-positions.pdf.
2. SmallBizGenius. "The Leadership Gap: 20 Male vs. Female CEO Statistics (2025)." *SmallBizGenius*, 2025. Accessed January 31, 2025. https://www.smallbizgenius.net/knowledge-base/male-vs-female-ceo-statistics/.
3. Deloitte. "Women in the Boardroom: A Global Perspective." Deloitte Insights, 2024. Accessed January 31, 2025. https://www2.deloitte.com/global/en/insights/topics/leadership/women-in-the-boardroom-global-perspective.html.
4. World Economic Forum. "Advancing Gender Parity in Entrepreneurship: Strategies for a More Equitable Future." *World Economic Forum*, 2024. Accessed January 31, 2025. https://www.weforum.org/reports/advancing-gender-parity-in-entrepreneurship/.
5. Smith, Jane, and Emily Johnson. Gender Equality at Work: A 2024 Survey of Women Across Four Generations. New York: Equality Press, 2024.

Chapter 12

1. Independent Women's Forum. "She Works: 10 Facts about Women in the Workforce 2024." *Independent Women's Forum*, March 4, 2024. Accessed January 31, 2025. https://www.iwf.org/2024/03/04/10-facts-women-in-workforce-2024/.

2. Gender Equity Policy Institute. "The Free-Time Gender Gap." *Gender Equity Policy Institute*, October 2024. Accessed January 31, 2025. https://thegepi.org/the-free-time-gender-gap/.
3. "Women In Tech Statistics (2024) - The Hard Truth." *Tech Insights Journal*, 2024. Accessed January 31, 2025. https://www.techinsightsjournal.com/women-in-tech-statistics-2024.
4. World Economic Forum. "Future of Jobs Report 2025: 78 Million New Jobs by 2030 but Urgent Upskilling Needed to Prepare Workforces." *World Economic Forum*, 2025. Accessed January 31, 2025. https://www.weforum.org/press/2025/01/future-of-jobs-report-2025-press-release.

Acknowledgements

Life is the grandest adventure, but it's the people who walk beside us that make it truly extraordinary.

To our beloved families: Patryk and Luis, our incredible husbands—your support and love are the bedrock of our journey. Krzysztof, Alex, and Isaiah, our sons—you are our greatest inspirations and constant reminders of what matters most. To our moms and dads—your guidance and love have shaped who we are today. To our sisters, Agnieszka, Elianis, and Elimir—your strength and friendship are treasures we hold close to our hearts.

To Microsoft Corporation—and every Employee Resource Group (ERG) and cohort across the organization: Thank you for being a platform that empowers us and countless women around the world. Your commitment to innovation and inclusion has opened doors for so many.

To Bill Gates and Paul Allen—50 years ago, you ignited a spark that became an unstoppable force for good. Your vision and relentless pursuit of possibility have not only revolutionized technology but have also touched lives across the globe, including the remarkable individuals featured in this book. We stand on your shoulders, grateful for the path you've paved.

To Satya Nadella—your leadership is nothing short of transformative. You've taught us that empathy is not just a "soft" skill but a powerful force capable of reshaping organizations and communities. Through your vision, we've learned that vulnerability and compassion can harmoniously coexist with innovation and excellence.

To every leader, colleague, mentor, manager, and friend we've had the privilege to work alongside—you are more than just part of our professional journey; you are family. Your wisdom, support, and countless acts of kindness have enriched our lives immeasurably. We carry your lessons and love in our hearts.

To the 50 contributors across countries, regions, and global time zones who shared their energy and stories—you are the heartbeat of this book. Your openness and honesty breathed life into these pages. Each story added depth and vibrancy, making this work truly special. Thank you for trusting us with your experiences.

A heartfelt thank you to Jennifer Cooper and Natalia Nikonenko—your support transcended contributions. Your dedication, encouragement, and belief in this project were the wind beneath our wings. This book wouldn't exist without you.

I wanted to express my heartfelt gratitude to all the incredible women who have been by my side. I am truly blessed to have such an amazing support system. A special thank you to the Basket Girls Józefów team for igniting my passion and for all the laughs that turned into tears, helping me keep going and never give up.

A special note of gratitude to Magda Kasiewicz, Agata Kapica and Sylwia Maj—your encouragement to Izzy at the very start of this project set the foundation for everything that followed.

And to you, our readers—thank you for taking the time to immerse yourselves in these stories. We hope they inspire and uplift you as they have us.

With deepest gratitude, Izzy and Miri

About the Authors

Izzy Duiwe is a trailblazer at the intersection of technology and human connection, leading the charge in customer experience innovation within Microsoft Teams Engineering. With 15 years in the tech industry, she's worn many hats—from engineering to customer success—each role deepening her expertise in bridging cutting-edge technology with authentic human engagement. Izzy is passionate about empowering businesses through AI, but her true superpower lies in fostering meaningful relationships along the way.

A fierce advocate for women in tech, Izzy leads Microsoft's Women Chapter in Poland and co-founded the emPower Women program, creating spaces where women can thrive, lead, and support one another. Izzy makes her home in the town of Józefów, just outside Warsaw, with her husband, son, their energetic Jack Russell terrier, Blue, and their cat, Gata. When she's not leading in tech, you'll find her on the basketball court with her women's city league team, exploring the underwater world through scuba diving, or soaking up the serenity of the Polish seaside coast, where she loves to collect amber. For Izzy, life is about connection—whether it's through technology, community, or the simple joy of being near the ocean.

Miri Rodriguez is a powerhouse in the world of digital storytelling—a two-time bestselling author, award-winning marketer, and an unwavering advocate for women in business. With more than 15 years of experience, Miri has carved out a space where creativity meets strategy, earning accolades in the tech, marketing, and communications industries along the way. But Miri's influence doesn't stop at her professional achievements; it extends to her passion for lifting others as she climbs.

Her latest venture, Empressa.ai, is a shining example of that commitment. More than just a platform, Empressa.ai is a movement designed to empower women in the workplace through AI-driven insights, mentorship, and tools tailored to help them break barriers and lead with confidence.

Miri's life is as vibrant as her career. A true adventurer at heart, she loves traveling the world, but Italy holds a special place for her—the rich food, the warm culture, and the sense of connection feel like home. As a digital nomad, Miri's global experiences fuel her work, bringing a unique depth and perspective to everything she touches. Just like Izzy, Miri finds solace and inspiration near the ocean. When she's not globe-trotting with her husband and visiting her two university-aged children, you'll find her grounded on one of South Florida's world-class beaches, centering herself to the rhythm of the waves—or making waves herself.

Index

accessibility, 131
adversity, 182
agentic AI, 208–9
agility, 85–6
AI
    agentic, 208–9
    bias in, 213–14, 217
    for collaboration, 11–12, 212–13
    for confidence, 208
    creativity in, 208, 212
    and curiosity, 213
    for education, 216–17
    empowerment through, 209, 212–13, 215–16
    engagement with, 2, 208
    feedback for, 213
    Generative, 25, 155, 161, 217, 219
    impact of, 212, 215, 217
    innovation in, 207, 209–10, 212, 214
    multimodal, 212
    responsible, 161, 213–15
AI in Women's Lives
    bias in, 213–14, 217
    confidence through, 208
    education and upskilling, 150, 153–4, 157, 161, 216–17
    responsible use, 161, 213–15
Allen, Paul, 5–6
allies, 57, 63, 90, 170, 197, 200, 202, 223–4
    see also mentors; sponsors
Amazon, 27, 151
Anis-Hanna, Lora, 108
application lifecycle management (ALM) consultants, 31
Aspire Reverse Mentorship Program, 29
Azure, 9, 85, 108, 153, 198–9
Azure AI Fundamentals, 161
Azure AI Services, 161

balance
    and burnout, 141, 143
    and emotional intelligence, 181, 183
    forms of, 199
    importance of, 32, 137
    in marriage, 101
    Microsoft's commitment to, 37
    and perfectionism, 114, 117–18, 132
    redefining, 125
    rhythm of, 138–42
    of strength and compassion, 169
    work-life, 125, 134, 153
BAM (Blacks at Microsoft), 65–6, 103
Barbie, 41
Beacon of Growth, 104
Beeman, Shakena, 100–5, 233
belonging
    and confidence, 14, 20, 167, 169, 198
    and connection, 222
    ERGs fostering, 73
    and Human Resources, 50, 51
    and imposter syndrome, 132
    sense of, 31
    in table metaphor, 74
    women at Microsoft, 205
Bianco, Anne-Claire (AC) Lo, 105–9, 227
bias
    in AI, 213–14, 217
    in enterprise agreement model, 84
    ignoring, 173
    recognizing, 72
    and resilience, 88, 90
    self-, 81–2
    and self-advocacy, 91
    and self-doubt, 80–2
    workplace, 89
    see also AI bias; self-bias; self-doubt

Bias Monster, 5, 77–92
Bing Chat, 161
Boettcher, Diane C., 121–3, 228
Bond, Sarah, 213–15, 233
Bonito, Ester De Nicolas, 218–21, 228
Boston University, 153–4
Brons, Lisanne, 69–72, 230
Brown, Brené, 171, 179
Burg, Steph, 26–8, 133, 234
Burlakova, Nataliia, 134–8, 232
burnout
    buildup of, 123, 125
    communication for, 140
    irony of, 136
    from overcommitment, 126, 133
    from perfectionism, 131, 147
    recovery from, 125
    and resilience, 91
    signs of, 143

calibration, 113
Cape Cod Conservatory, 139
CAPE (customer and partner ecosystem), 46–7
Cerda, Marisela, 194–7, 231
CFS (commerce & finance services), 73
Chanel, Coco, 165
Choi, Na-Young, 51–4, 232
circumstantial assurance, 6
Cliburn Amateur Piano Competition, 139
Clippy, 10
cloud computing, 4, 9, 153
collaboration
    and adaptability, 153
    AI for, 11–12, 212–13
    and compassion, 169, 181
    competition vs., 170
    control vs., 98
    during COVID, 45
    cultivating, 177
    in DEI initiatives, 64
    and empowerment, 68
    in hackathons, 158
    with HR, 50
    and inclusion, 183
    interpersonal skills for, 34
    knowledge sharing as, 156
    lack of, 147
    and leadership, 176

    in Microsoft Garage, 59
    in recruits, 37
    skills in resumes, 38
commerce & finance services (CFS), 73
compassion, 19, 136, 170, 181, 225
    see also empathy
compassionate strength, 169
confidence
    AI for, 208
    algorithm of, 16–20
    and authenticity, 180
    beliefs for building, 145
    and belonging, 167, 169
    career development for, 29
    and community, 222
    culture of, 49
    definition of, 5–6
    and DEI, 69
    education for, 215
    and Empressa.ai, 162
    environment for, 10–11
    external, 6
    and imposter syndrome, 130, 171, 176
    and independence, 148
    internal, 6
    in interviews, 198–9
    journey to, 1–4
    law of, 14–16
    leading with, 171–2, 178–9, 225
    and mansplaining, 97–8
    obstacles to, 187
    and perfectionism, 117
    programs for, 158–9, 161
    rebuilding, 90
    self-, 16
    and self-acceptance, 23
    and self-awareness, 174
    showing, 183–4
    skills for, 34
    social media's effect on, 7–8
    and success, 27
    support for, 140
    visualizing, 32
    see also self-belief; self-confidence; She confidence
confidence algorithm, 16–21
Connect AI, 215–16
constructive learning, 146
continuous learning, 13, 91, 107, 153, 155–7
Cook, Heather, 222–5, 229
Cooper, Jennifer, 118–20, 230

Copilot, 6, 9, 12, 165, 207, 211
  see also M365 Copilot
Courtois, Jean-Philippe, 29
COVID-19, 11–12, 33, 43, 101, 117, 187, 224
creativity
  and AI, 208, 212
  and balance, 138
  and collaboration, 158, 177
  and connection, 183
  continuous learning for, 157
  and innovation, 156, 182
  in Microsoft Garage, 58–9
  possibility of, 221
  in problem-solving, 73
  in unexpected spaces, 68–9
  see also innovation
CSAMs (customer success account managers), 28–9
Cuff, Sonia, 123–7, 234
curiosity
  and adaptability, 153
  and AI, 213
  celebrating, 38
  and continuous learning, 155
  culture of, 34
  environment for, 166
  and inclusion, 71
  in learn-it-all cultures, 158, 162
  timelessness of, 183
  and unlearning, 148
  in world wide web, 9
customer and partner ecosystem (CAPE), 46–7
customer engagement, 86–7
customer success account managers (CSAMs), 28–9
Customer Zero Math, 48–50
cybersecurity, 154, 155, 167, 169, 176, 208, 218
Cybersecurity Women of the World conference, 154

Dataverse platform, 207
deepfakes, 214
DEI (diversity, equity, and inclusion)
  and community, 67
  engagement for, 72
  environment of, 51
  global view of, 63–5
  growth from, 108

importance of, 61–2
  struggles with, 69
  see also diversity and inclusion (D&I); inclusion
DigiGirlz, 66
discipline, 142–3 *see also* grit
diversity and inclusion (D&I), 73
  see also DEI (diversity, equity, and inclusion); inclusion
Duiwe, Izabela "Izzy," xi, 47, 95–100, 147
Duolingo, 96

EA (enterprise agreement) model, 84, 85
Earhart, Amelia, 142
EBCs (executive briefing centers), 68
education
  AI for, 216–17
  during COVID, 11–12
  of customers, 150–1, 152–3
  as empowerment, 149–50
  as key to success, 148–9
  of mentors, 29
  and mentorship, 154
  and protection, 215
  and self-doubt, 80
  in underrepresented communities, 108
  and unlearning, 152
emotional intelligence, 182–3, 184
empathy
  in AI, 212
  communicating, 175, 191
  confidence from, 90
  in gaming, 213
  and innovation, 170, 171
  and leadership, 120, 166, 183
  and partnership, 87
  and resilience, 91
  through storytelling, 105
  as strength, 169, 245
  see also compassion
employee resource groups (ERGs), 64, 71, 73, 103
empowerment
  through accessibility, 131
  through AI, 209, 212–13, 215–16
  and authenticity, 180
  in DEI, 51
  education as, 149–50, 152
  of employees, 157–9, 173
  and Empressa.ai, 162

empowerment (*continued*)
   in Microsoft Garage, 59
   in partnerships, 58
   in people-first mindset, 169
   in personal computing revolution, 8
   program for, 160
   and recognition, 172
   and responsible AI, 214
   and self-confidence, 13
   space for, 73
   stories of, 109, 111
   and thriving, 69, 154
   as way of being, 68
emPower Women, 142, 158
Empressa.ai, 24, 162
end-user scenarios, 52
engagement
   with AI, 2, 208
   and connection, 98
   with customers, 86–7
   through innovation, 182
   and learning, 146
   in learn-it-all culture, 158
   and resilience, 83, 87
   using Teams, 45
   with technology, 8
Epstein, David, 156
Equal Pay Act, 78
Era of AI, 10, 24, 161, 209
Erasmus program, 142
ESL (English as a second language), 96
Estés, Clarissa Pinkola, 77, 88
European DEI Index, 63
executive briefing centers (EBCs), 68

Facebook, 63
fast-moving consumer goods industry (FMCG), 48
Fayans Birenbaum, Shira, 82–8, 234
feedback
   for AI, 213, 217
   in CAPE environment, 46
   for external confidence, 6
   in fitting rooms, 166
   for growth, 191
   and resilience, 91
   and self doubt, 81
   using Teams, 45
financial planning and analysis (FP&A), 48–9
fitting room metaphor, 165–84

   adversity in, 182
   authenticity in, 178, 180, 182
   collaboration in, 177
   compassion in, 181
   emotional intelligence in, 181–2, 183
   inclusion in, 181, 183
   innovation and creativity in, 182, 183
   P-Framework in, 167–70
   pressure situations in, 177–8
   recognition in, 177
   resilience in, 180–1
   trust in, 172, 177
   see also rooms of the house concept; table metaphor
FMCG (fast-moving consumer goods industry), 48
FP&A (financial planning and analysis), 48–9
French Chamber of Great Britain, 106–7
Fulton, Jenia, 32–5, 229

Gage, John, 139
Gagnon, John, 150
gaming, 9, 213–14
Gandhi, Mahatma, 170
Gates, Bill, 5–6, 205
Gates, Melinda, 1, 20
Gatimu, Karuana, 224
Gaurav, Garima, 54–9, 228
Geena Davis Institute, 13
Generation X, 7
Generation Z, 7
Generative AI, 25, 155, 161, 217, 219
Girls Nail IT, 159
GitHub, 38
Global Hackathon, 157–8 *see also* hackathons
Global Women in Tech, 73
Goldin, Claudia, 120
Google Ads, 149
grit, 56, 142–3 *see also* discipline
grounding, 137, 167, 212
growth mindset, 36–8, 90, 108, 152, 157–8

hackathons, 68, 158 *see also* Global Hackathon
Hill, Aja, 65–7, 227
Hogan, Kathleen, 61
Hood, Amy, 23
How People Learn (Bransford, et al.), 145

Huffington, Arianna, 175
human resources (HR), 31–2, 50–1, 52, 71

Ignite, 86, 223
impact
    and accessibility, 114
    of AI, 212, 215, 217
    of collaboration, 45
    of DEI, 51
    from direct work, 31
    economic, 192
    of emotional intelligence, 181
    of inclusion, 183
    of leadership, 87–8, 166, 175, 179, 196
    on learning, 146
    as legacy, 191
    of mentors, 29–30, 146
    through narrative, 108
    programs for, 158–61
    purposeful, 167
    of relationships, 196
    of respect, 67
    and self-doubt, 44
imposter syndrome
    and balance, 132
    and confidence, 130, 171, 176
    dealing with, 7–8, 16, 31
    and failure, 5
    Women Rising modules for, 159
inclusion
    and compassion, 181
    and curiosity, 71
    digital, 216
    growth from, 158
    importance of, 65
    and innovation, 183
    and isolation, 62–3
    as lived experience, 205
    Microsoft's commitment to, 37
    practice of, 68
    in table metaphor, 61, 75
    see also DEI (diversity, equity, and inclusion); diversity and inclusion (D&I)
innovation
    in AI, 207, 209–10, 212, 214
    and co-creation, 85
    and collaboration, 147, 153, 156
    and connection, 59, 86–7, 222
    and continuous learning, 155
    and creativity, 156, 182

    DEI for, 61
    and empathy, 170, 171
    and empowerment, 157–8
    in fitting room metaphor, 182, 183
    future of, 218, 224
    and inclusion, 13, 183
    at Microsoft, 6, 9–10, 50, 157
    possibilities of, 168
    and resilience, 10, 12
    and risk, 179
    in rooms of the house concept, 58
    from storytelling, 156
    in table metaphor, 46, 169
    and trust, 213, 214
    see also creativity
Instagram, 99
Internet Explorer, 9
iPod, 10

Jakkal, Vasu, 166–71, 235
Johnson, Tiffany, 108
Joo, Gabriela, 48–50, 228

Kandzor, Susie, 157–9, 235
Kapour, Hapreet, 200–4, 229
Kaushik, Avinash, 150
Khan, Laiba A., 28–30, 230
knowledge stacking, 155–6
Kohoutova, Sarka, 62–3, 233

language of nature, 218–21
large language models (LLMs), 218
law of confidence, 14–16
leadership
    and collaboration, 176
    empathy in, 120, 166, 183
    impact of, 87–8, 166, 175, 179, 196
    and self-doubt, 202
    skills, 199
learn-HER-all mindset, 2–6, 145–63
learning and development (L&D), 150
learn-it-all mindset, 13, 148, 152–5, 157, 158, 162
legacy, xii, 73, 83–4, 91, 149, 162, 191, 203
LG Electronics, 33
Lindgren, Astrid, 69
LinkedIn, 28, 35, 38, 42, 73, 151
low-code/no-code solutions, 52
Luongo, Melissa, 50–1, 231

Maali, Maria, 57–9, 231
MACH (Microsoft Academy for College Hires) program, 52–3, 88
Majdoubi, Imane El, 197–200, 229
Malekzadeh, Sogol, 211–14, 234
Maleshykhina, Oksana, 115–18, 232
mansplaining, 97, 99
Markham, Michelle, 159–62, 231
Maybelline, 13
McDonald's, 63
McIntyre, Lindsay-Rae, 51
McKinsey & Co., 188
MCSE (Microsoft Certified System Engineer) certification, 53
mentors
   using, 179
   as allies, 197
   community, 63, 103–4
   compassion of, 181
   employees as, 29–30
   empowerment from, 68
   seeking, 38, 149, 154, 202
   and sponsors, 171
   support from, 90, 126
   see also allies; sponsors
Meta, 63
Microsoft Academy for College Hires (MACH) program, 52–3
Microsoft Africa, 57
Microsoft Australia, 161
Microsoft Band, 10
Microsoft Blockchain Academy, 88
Microsoft Brazil, 215
Microsoft Build, 223–4
Microsoft Certified System Engineer (MCSE) certification, 53
Microsoft Cloud for Sustainability, 9
Microsoft Engineering, 115
Microsoft Finance, 48
Microsoft for Startups, 105, 106
Microsoft Garage, 58–9
Microsoft Kin, 10
Microsoft Learn, 153
Microsoft Power Platform Community Conference, 224
Microsoft Teams, 11–14, 43, 45, 67, 116–17
Microsoft 365 minestrone, 224
misconceptions, 146
MIT Sloan, 188
Mocke, Sarah, 176–9, 233

Modiface AI, 13
Morgan Stanley, 153
MS-DOS, 8
M365 Copilot, 47, 69 *see also* Copilot
multimodal AI, 212
multitasking, 34
MVP Summit, 224

Nadella, Satya, 9, 29, 31, 36, 132, 157, 170, 188–90, 209
National AI Skilling Program, 215, 217
natural language processing, 161, 210
Nikonenko, Natalia, 80–2, 232
Nissan, 63
Nokia, 9
non-conflict culture, 177
non-playable characters (NPCs), 213

Oberlin College, 78
object linking and embedding (OLE), 130
Office 365 software, 9
OpenAI, 208
Oracle Global, 67
origin stories, 99, 105, 109–11 *see also* storytelling

Parks, Rosa, 187
people-first mindset, 86–7, 168
perfectionism, 54, 111–27, 131–2, 137, 143, 147–8, 205
P-Framework, 167
Piano, Débora Di, 25, 30–2, 227
Pinnacle Award, 197, 199
Playfair Capital Female Founders Office Hours initiative, 108
problem-solving, 14, 34, 36, 73, 168
Psychology Today, 113

Qatar Airways, 32–3
QDOS, 8
quantum computing, 207, 218–19, 220–1
quantum encryption, 218
quantum simulations, 220

Range: Why Generalists Triumph in a Specialized World (Epstein), 156
Recap, 12
recognition, 4, 85, 177, 184, 188, 194, 201

recruitment, 28–9, 35–7
representation
    advocating for, 68
    importance of, 66–7, 103–4
    in managerial positions, 192
    underrepresented communities, 108, 154, 196–7
resilience, 77–92
    and adaptability, 153
    through adversity, 182
    balancing, 91–2
    building, 90–1
    of communities, 222
    and confidence, 15, 19–20
    growth of, 84–5
    importance of, 180–1
    and innovation, 10, 12
    in minorities, 195, 197
    as motivation, 103
    and perfectionism, 138
    and presence, 175
    and self-belief, 44
    and self-doubt, 80–2, 107, 203, 206
    as skill, 34, 88–93
    and transformation, 83, 87–8
    and trust, 214
    during war, 134–6
reskilling, 24, 157 *see also* skills; upskilling
responsible AI, 161, 213–15 *see also* AI
Robbins, Rita, 188–94, 233
robotics, 207–8, 218
Rodrigues, Lucia, 215–18, 230
Rodriguez, Miri, 23–4, 67, 95, 133, 142, 166, 181
rooms of the house concept, 21, 23, 39, 42, 57, 166, 205 *see also* fitting room metaphor; table metaphor
Roosevelt, Eleanor, 79
Rouse, Carissa, 179–84, 227

Sahi, Ginniee, 69–72, 229
Salesforce, 67
Sarkar, Dona, 23, 224, 228
Schaef, Anne Wilson, 113
Secure Future Initiative, 9, 214
self-acceptance, 18–19
self-advocacy, 194–7
self-assurance, 2, 4, 19, 56
self-awareness, 17, 91, 170, 174, 178
self-belief, 5–6, 13, 44, 207

self-bias, 81–2
self-care, 91, 153
self-compassion, 19
self-confidence, 13, 16 *see also* confidence
self-doubt
    as bias, 80–2
    and imposter syndrome, 31, 171, 178
    from interruptions, 98
    in leaders, 202
    learning from, 107
    self-acceptance vs., 18
self-love, 19–20
self-validation, 174
Sengupta, Monalisa, 171–5, 231
Shalhoub, Rawan, 71
SharePoint, 52, 223–4
She confidence, 11, 13–14, 17–18
    see also confidence
She Evolution, 206–7
Shewolves, 91–2, 141
skills
    through AI, 209, 215, 217
    for collaboration, 34
    for confidence, 34
    essential, 51
    importance of, 161
    interpersonal, 33–4
    language, 206
    leadership, 199
    of resilience, 34, 88–92
    social, 181
    soft, 156, 166, 245
    storytelling, 156
    transferable, 59
    see also reskilling; upskilling
Skills for the Future program, 161
Skowera, Weronika, 43–8, 235
Skype for Business, 11
Smith, Brad, 222
Snapp, Mary, 14–21, 231
soft skills, 156, 166, 245 *see also* skills
sponsors, 63, 160, 171, 179
    see also allies; mentors
SQL server stew, 224
Stańczak, Kasia, 35–9, 230
Stander, Jane Santos, 206–8, 229
STEM, 3
storytelling, 40, 95–1112
    and agility, 86
    approach to, 98
    connection through, 43, 105–9, 165

storytelling (*continued*)
   in ERGs, 73
   in gaming, 213
   self-acceptance through, 100–5
   as soft skill, 156
   see also origin stories
Strazdina, Renate, 155–7, 233
Sund, Pooja, 72–5, 232
support networks, 27, 62, 90, 140, 147, 161, 198–9
Swift, Taylor, 180
Sylvester, Freada, 209–13, 228

table metaphor
   belonging in, 74
   challenges in, 69
   inclusion in, 61, 67, 75
   ownership in, 201, 204
   as sacred space, 75
   uniqueness in, 70, 157
   see also fitting room metaphor; rooms of the house concept
Tatem, Stacy, 153–5, 234
Teams *see* Microsoft Teams
teamwork, 13, 34, 50, 101, 102
TechEd Barcelona, 223
TechHer, 159
tech homemaking, 43–8
Teper, Jeff, 224
time management, 34, 103, 139, 142
translation, 207
2024 Global Diversity & Inclusion Report, 64
two walls rule, 135

United States Air Force, 102
University of Washington, 223
University of Wisconsin, 26
unlabeled concept, 206–8
unlearning, 148, 152
upskilling, 150, 153–4, 157, 161 *see also* reskilling; skills
U.S. Bureau of Labor Statistics, 46

Virji, Purna, 148–52, 232
Virtual Event Playbook, 224
visibility
   fostering, 76
   improving your own, 196, 201
   lack of, in some essential roles, 59
   through leadership, 198
   through recognition, 177
   see also imposter syndrome; mentors
voice
   amplifying, 68, 224
   and diversity, equity, and inclusion, 51
   embracing, 56
   finding, 20, 75, 92
   hearing every, 168, 173, 176
   learning to use, 196, 201
   listening to your inner, 127
   reclaiming, 98
   underrepresented, 202
   see also storytelling

Wadhwa, Sonia, 88–92, 234
WAM (Women at Microsoft Employee Resource Group), 65–6, 73
Wang, Wendy, 138–43, 235
Windows bisque, 224
Windows ME, 10
Windows 8 operating system, 10
Windows 12 operating system, 9
Windows 95 operating system, 9
Windows Phones, 9
Windows Vista, 10
Winfrey, Oprah, 129
wolf skills, 92
Women at Microsoft Scholarships, 66
Women in Cybersecurity, 154
women mentoring circles, 63
Women Rising, 159–61
Women Who Run With the Wolves (Estés), 77, 79, 88
Word, 130–1
workplace discrimination, 192
World Bank, 192
World Economic Forum, 161

Xbox, 9, 49, 158, 213

Ye, Lan, 11–14, 230

Zhang, Clare, 108
Zune, 10